YOU CAN BE
THE WIFE OF A
HAPPY
HUSBAND

 Discovering the Keys to Marital Success

DARIEN B. COOPER

DESTINY IMAGE® PUBLISHERS, INC.
P.O. Box 310, Shippensburg, PA 17257-0310
"Speaking to the Purposes of God for This Generation and for the Generations to Come."

This book and all other Destiny Image, Revival Press, MercyPlace, Fresh Bread, Destiny Image Fiction, and Treasure House books are available at Christian bookstores and distributors worldwide.

For a U.S. bookstore nearest you, call 1-800-722-6774.
For more information on foreign distributors, call 717-532-3040.
Reach us on the Internet: www.destinyimage.com.

ISBN 13 Trade Paper: 978-0-7684-3601-3
ISBN 13 Hardcover: 978-0-7684-3602-0
ISBN 13 Large Print: 978-0-7684-3603-7
ISBN 13 Ebook: 978-0-7684-9051-0

For Worldwide Distribution, Printed in the U.S.A.
1 2 3 4 5 6 7 / 13 12 11

Dedication

To my beloved DeWitt.

Acknowledgments

I am deeply indebted to so many for the birth and revisions of this book. Thank you to Patricia Bradley, Anna Stanley, Phyllis Ott, and Grace Fox for their valuable contributions to the original manuscript.

Thank you, Stephen Sorenson and Mary McNeil and her team for the strategic work that brought about the revisions in 2005.

To the DI editing team, I say thank you for the expanded revisions and updates in this 2010 release.

My gratitude to my husband, DeWitt, and our family members who have given their enthusiastic cooperation and support during the 36-year journey this book has traveled.

I appreciate the scores of women who have permitted me to use their experiences as illustrations (disguised, of course, to conceal identities).

I also want to thank the following women who graciously shared with me their testimonies of reading this book.

℘ I started at Ground Zero. As a new bride just coming back to the Lord I entered my second marriage with five children between us. I never studied God's word or knew that He had a plan for my marriage. I thought you just get married and if it works great, if not, suffer through it until the next divorce. Through this study and working through various issues, we are enjoying the kind of fulfilling relationship God desires for every married couple. I now have complete peace and satisfaction in my marriage, regardless of the circumstances!

❧ I began doing the things this book said to do and within weeks I began to feel good about myself. This was the major problem in our marriage. The results have been amazing. I quit trying to change my husband and just thank God for him.

❧ The leader of one Happy Husband class said that an 82-year-old woman attended because she was lonely and wanted to be around people. Even though she had been a Christian for 50 years, she said no one ever told her these truths. She says that she has learned so much. New excitement has entered her life and she is thinking about looking for a new husband to try out everything she's learned.

❧ I read your book and God showed me areas within me that were destructive. I called my ex-husband and we dated and went to Bible study together. We were remarried a few months later after being divorced for seven years.

❧ God used the principles in this book to help me realize that my security is in God and to have the peace that endures and passes all understanding. Our 59 years of marriage became a fulfilling reality.

❧ I am married to a 'difficult man.' However, the closer I walk with my Lord, I have noticed the closer my husband draws to me. It is a mystical, but beautiful relationship. I have learned to separate myself from his 'negative' statements and outlook. I am learning to see my worth in myself as one of God's children.

- I am happier and freer than ever before. I feel like the weight of the world has been lifted from me.

- Our marriage has improved 100 percent. We are working together as a team. The best part is that once I started living my faith, the results were fast.

Contents

Foreword

Darien Cooper is a real woman—satisfied and fulfilled. It did not take her three or four marriages to discover what it takes to please a man. She discovered that secret the first time around and is practicing what she teaches.

At least four men love and admire this woman: her husband and their three sons. Hundreds of women attend her two weekly Bible classes, where she expounds the principles found in this book. Many troubled wives have been brought into her classes by friends and have gone away transformed by the principles they have learned there. A number of these women have changed from competitor to partner, much to the amazement of their husbands.

I first met Darien when I went to Atlanta, Georgia, to hold a Family Life Seminar. She and her husband, DeWitt, met my wife and me at the Atlanta airport. I was excited when I heard how God was using Darien, but I was even more impressed with the way her husband shared her enthusiasm about her ministry.

Any time I find a man who takes genuine pride in what his wife does outside the home, I know she must be a wise woman. It's natural for a man to feel threatened by his partner's success. Not so with DeWitt. He is thrilled that God is using Darien to help wives experience satisfying relationships with their husbands.

It is about time a woman says some of the things Darien expresses in this book. She has an excellent grasp of the biblical concepts that produce happiness in marriage and states them clearly. She knows that a woman is not some weak, brainless creature a man marries only for erotic pleasure or to display as an ornament. Instead, she sees a woman as an absolute essential to a man's fulfillment in life. But she is vitally aware that a wife must accept her God-given role, or she will ruin the partnership.

Darien Cooper has a thorough understanding of the male ego. In this book, she discusses the biblical principles every wife needs to know in order to live with that ego. Many family explosions could be avoided if more wives knew these secrets. Hopefully, thousands of women who may never have a chance to hear Darien speak will read this book and find God's help for their marriages.

Tim LaHaye

Preface

Darien did not have to write a book to become a good wife. It did however clear up a lot of problems with the way I was raised. Coming from the mountains of Tennessee, my idea of a wife was to obey my commands without question. This went great until it didn't work anymore. Through the book and many sessions, our life and marriage gets better and better. We still have some attitudes, but we are able to solve them.

The plaque that I gave Darien on our 50th anniversary is a good summary of our marriage.

In remembrance of 50 years
August 24, 1957-2007
We have fought the good fight
We are finishing the course
We have kept the faith.

But we must let our
Endurance come to it's perfect
Product so we can be
Fully developed and
Perfectly equipped without
Any defects.

DeWitt Cooper

Introduction

You can find your true identity by discovering God's role for you as a woman and a wife. This book is designed to help you make those discoveries.

I believe God has given us women the choice role. Unfortunately, many of us do not realize that being a woman and a wife are wonderful privileges, so we miss the joy and fulfillment God has in store for us. Although we want happiness, some of us back off after being exposed to the biblical principles and concepts explained in this book. We say, "This is too good to be true," or "It won't work for me," or as I once said, "You have to be kidding. I don't need help."

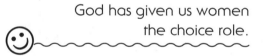

God has given us women
the choice role.

At that time, I wasn't teachable. If you had asked me if I had any personal problems, I would have replied, "Nothing serious; nothing that needs changing. But my husband—now that's a different story!" I thought I had a good marriage, but as I look back now, I realize I simply had a good man. For 12 years, I tried to change DeWitt—the way he did things or didn't do them, or the way he related to me. I tried direct approaches and subtle ones. I'd cry when he forgot my birthday or our anniversary. I'd wonder why he wouldn't put his arms around me and tell me he was sorry and loved me. It seemed as if the more I cried, the less attention he gave me.

One day I said, "DeWitt, I've been watching the Joneses next door. Mr. Jones is so thoughtful. He brings his wife candy and flowers. He always kisses her affectionately at the door when he comes home from work. Why don't you do that?"

"Because I don't know her that well," he responded. (Even though this is a joke, it accurately portrays how he and I have often misunderstood each other, resulting in conflict and pain. However, in God's hands our oppositeness has been transformational!)

I'd listen to what he'd tell me when he came home from work and give him unsolicited advice on what he should or should not have said or done. I couldn't understand why he didn't seem to appreciate my input and eventually stopped mentioning work-related experiences.

Then one day, after an intensive study of the Bible, I realized that God provides definite solutions to life's problems—including a detailed outline of how a successful marriage may be maintained. I discovered that instead of helping DeWitt, I had been crushing him—destroying his masculinity. "OK, God," I prayed, "I'm ready for You to show me how to be the kind of wife I should be."

Today, after I have worked through various issues and developed a stronger relationship with both God and DeWitt, he and I are enjoying a fulfilling relationship, which God desires for every married couple. Life has become exciting as I apply biblical principles God shows me. I've found that I can have complete peace and satisfaction in my marriage, regardless of circumstances.

> God provides definite solutions to life's problems—including a detailed outline of how a successful marriage may be maintained.

God is no respecter of persons. His truth is for all who believe, who put their faith in Jesus Christ. All you need is a teachable attitude—the willingness to let God work in your life. As you trust God and obey His Word, you will find—as I and so many other women have—the fulfillment you want and more.

I wrote this book in order to share with as many women as possible the truths that have transformed my life and marriage. My only regret is that I did not learn and apply these principles sooner and more perfectly as the years progressed. It is important that you read this book in the sequence in which it is written because each chapter builds on previous ones. Please try to withhold judgment on any single truth I present until you've read the whole book. As you study these principles, remember that they apply whether or not your husband is a believer in Jesus Christ.

As you put these principles into practice and make them a way of life, you should see changes in your husband as well as in yourself. It has been exciting for me to hear about and see firsthand the reactions of husbands who don't know that their wives are studying God's plan for a happy marriage relationship. Many husbands cannot understand why their wives have suddenly become sweeter or easier to live with.

Keep in mind, however, that these kinds of changes take time, so be patient and let God "do the changing." Rely on Him to build or rebuild your marriage. *"Unless the Lord builds the house, its builders labor in vain..."* (Ps. 127:1).

I also suggest that you purchase a notebook and make your own journal/workbook as you read this book. Jot down in one column the attitudes and habits Jesus speaks to your heart that need to be changed. Ask God to show you creative steps you can take to change each wrong attitude or habit, then list these steps in the opposite column. As God leads, try out these ideas. Answer the questions at the end of the book in the Reader's Guide after each chapter in your notebook. Add your prayer requests with the dates. You will be encouraged as you look back later and see the changes God has made.

I pray that through this book you will discover the full, satisfying life God has for you as a woman and a wife, and I pray that you'll become the wife your husband needs. To put it another way, I pray that you will become "the happy wife of a happy husband."

Said another way, may you become the real woman God designed you to be. From the beginning of this book, I would have chosen the title, Will the Real Woman Please Stand Up? For me these truths were about becoming the woman I was designed to be as God used my marital relationship as a transformational tool in His hand. If I saw results in my marriage, that was a bonus. Either way, it was a win-win situation!

1

The Perfect Plan

One warm afternoon in Valdosta, Georgia, Margie Maultsby, an attractive woman in her 30s, was seriously planning her future apart from her husband, Joe. Although they had been reunited for six months following a separation she had forced, their life together had not improved. The next day, a casual acquaintance invited Margie to attend a neighborhood Bible class featuring my recorded messages on biblical principles from this book.

Years later, during a visit in my home, Margie vulnerably shared the miraculous way God had worked. She said when she was invited to the class she thought, "What can this white woman teach this black woman that could help my hopeless marriage?" Then she continued, "Darien, not only did I not intend to go to the class, I do not remember getting ready to go, or traveling to the host's house. All I remember was standing at her door knocking." We rejoiced over the awesome ways of our God as we reveled in the immediate oneness God gave us as sisters in Christ. We felt that we had known each other all of our lives.

Margie's letters to God, written after the first and second sessions respectively, reveal her heart:

Dear God,

Can You believe I attended that Bible class? Don't ask me why! Before I knew anything, I was ringing that doorbell, introducing myself to the Bible-class leader and hostess, and taking a seat among ten other strangers.

Did I enjoy the class? I don't know; I can't remember too much. However, I do have homework. This is ludicrous; I have enough schoolwork to do as it is. After all, Father, I am an English teacher. I really don't have time for this; I probably won't go again. That lady on the cassette tape can't tell me anything that I don't know. I've read lots of material on marriages. I'm still trying to apply some of those principles. My marriage is OK anyway. It's about as good as most. Everybody has problems. Anyway, I don't want to think about marriage; I want to think about You and Christ.

Margie

Dear God,

I'm still in a state of shock after last night in that ladies' Bible class! Yes, I went again!

Well, I received quite a blow; it was truly a bolt! I discovered that I didn't really love my husband. Can You believe this? I couldn't. I thought I had always been a good wife. However, when I began to listen to the words from First Corinthians 13:4-7 for the first time, those words describing love began to have some merit—"**is kind, not jealous, thinks no evil, seeks not her own, believes all things, hopes all things, endures all things.**" I realized that I am kind to Joe only when he does what I want him to do. I've got a lot to learn!

You see, God, I am actually jealous! At night, I search Joe's wallet. I also check his stories when he comes home so that I can make sure that he is telling the truth. How else would I know? Sometimes I wait up for him just to attack him with threatening words and accusations. At these times, I am constantly thinking evil. I have looked at Joe for so long; I had no idea that my mirror held so much evil.

In addition to all that has been said, heavenly Father, I seek my own way. I never really give any thought to Joe's dreams; I'm only interested in mine. I never let him be free to think, to plan, or to dream. I try only to make my values his values. You see, Joe belongs to a club, and I'm always afraid that if he behaves badly at a nightclub or if he stays out too late that someone may think less of me or even less of my marriage. Stupid, I know. However, for this reason, I have always tried to get him to watch his behavior. Not only is this wrong according to Your Word, but it doesn't work anyway. If I lecture for a long time or if I become angry and threaten to leave him, he does seem to behave according to my standards for a while.

During these times, I am on top of the world. Then boom! Back to his same old habits. I should have known something was wrong, but I didn't. I thought this was just the way to live. Then I read, **"Except the Lord build the house, they labor in vain who build it"** (Ps. 127:1). I give You my house to build. Father, teach me how to love my husband.

Margie

After the second class, Margie placed her life and marriage completely into God's hands. She began dying to her old ways and in turn was free to love God's way. During the next difficult year, Jesus gave her the strength to love Joe unconditionally. Shortly thereafter, with much tenderness and a new consideration for Margie, Joe said, "I want the Lord to give me a portion of what you have."

She and Joe now enjoy a new love for each other and the marital fulfillment that God wants to give all couples. God has also used Margie mightily to teach others in the town where she lives.

A Satisfying Life

God did not create you and put you on this earth to live an apathetic, frustrated, defeated, or discouraged life. He meant for you to be happier than you ever dreamed possible.

> *Now glory be to God who by his mighty power at work within us is able to do far more than we would ever dare to ask or even dream of—infinitely beyond our highest prayers, desires, thoughts, or hopes* (Ephesians 3:20 TLB).

Jesus Christ said that He came to provide a satisfying, complete life for you and me. He came that we *"may have life, and have it to the full"* (John 10:10).

God did not create you and
put you on this earth to live
an apathetic, frustrated, defeated,
or discouraged life.

This life is available to you regardless of your background, education, nationality, or present circumstances. There is no problem too large or too small for Christ to work out in your life. All that He requires from you is a willing heart and obedience to His plan. *"If you are willing and obedient, you will eat the best from the land"* (Isa. 1:19). The *"best from the land"* can be compared to an abundant life for you.

A Personalized Plan

God loves you so much that He has worked out a personal plan for you so that you will experience growth, development, and fulfillment. You might think of your life as a divine prescription from His hand. Consider these words written by the psalmist David:

> *You made all the delicate, inner parts of my body, and knit them together in my mother's womb. Thank you for making me so wonderfully complex! It is amazing to think about. Your workmanship is marvelous—and how well I know it. You were there while I was being formed in utter seclusion! You saw me before I was born and scheduled each day of my life before I began to breathe. Every day was recorded in your Book!*

> *How precious it is, Lord, to realize that you are thinking about me constantly! I can't even count how many times a day your thoughts turn towards me. And when I waken in the morning, you are still thinking of me* (Psalm 139:13-18 TLB).

God cares so much for you that He is always thinking about you and watching everything that concerns you. No accidents occur in the lives of God's children.

He desires to use your personality, physical body, and background to your advantage.

If you trust Him, He can take all the things in your life that you would like to change and work them out for your ultimate good. The apostle Paul wrote, *"We know that in all things God works for the good of those who love Him, who have been called according to His purpose"* (Rom. 8:28). Notice that he did not say that all things are good, but that God will work out all things for your good. Only He can perform such miracles.

> If you trust Him, He can take all the things in your life that you would like to change and work them out for your ultimate good.

It's true that not everything will always seem to work out for your good here on earth, at least from your perspective. You will no doubt face difficulties and challenges, and so will your loved ones. But do not resist what God is doing. Simply trust Him to know what is best for you. *"Who are you...to talk back to God? Shall what is formed say to Him who formed it, 'Why did you make me like this?'"* (Rom. 9:20). There may be behaviors and attitudes that you do not like about yourself or your mate. Rather than trying to change them in the way that seems right to you, you are to discover and accept God's plan for your life so that He can work out all things to your ultimate good.

MARRIAGE—A FULFILLING RELATIONSHIP

Everything God has designed for us is for our ultimate benefit. This includes marriage. The marriage relationship is the most intimate of all earthly relationships. It is to mirror our relationship with Christ. We learn to give and receive love, helping each other to be all we are designed to be. In the meantime, we learn who we are and how to enjoy being ourselves.

Think about these words from the book of Ephesians:

Submit to one another out of reverence for Christ. Wives, submit to your husbands as to the Lord. ... Husbands, love your wives, just as Christ loved the church and gave himself up for her....In this same way, husbands ought to love their wives as their own bodies. He who loves his wife loves himself. After all, no one ever hated his own body, but he feeds and cares for it, just as Christ does the church....However, each one of you also must love his wife as he loves himself, and the wife must respect and reverence her husband" (Ephesians 5: 21-22, 25, 28-29, 33).

Notice that submission is for both marital partners. The husband submits by loving his wife. The wife submits by respecting and reverencing her husband.

I believe the role of the wife in the marital relationship is the choice role. We are to be loved, protected, and cherished by our husbands in the same way that Christ gave Himself for the Church (all believers).

In recent years, the word *submission* has created much conflict and misunderstanding among women. There are many reasons for this: the rise of feminist thinking, the false linking of biblical submission to women whose husbands are abusing them, the increasing number of women who have chosen to enter the workplace and work alongside men, and so forth.

Rather than spending many pages on this topic, I'd like to share some principles that, in addition to being biblical, have helped many women—myself included—understand our roles in marriage and thereby be able to reflect who God wants us to be in our marriages.

The words *submit to* describe the way you and I are to relate to our husbands. Another way of saying this is that we are to be responders to our hubands' love, protection, and leadership. Submission never means that our personalities, abilities, talents, or individuality should be buried. Rather, they are to be directed so they can be maximized and reflect the goodness and glory of God.

> We are to be responders to our husband's love, protection, and leadership.

Matthew Henry wrote, "Woman was created from man, not from his head to be commanded by him, nor from his feet to be his slave. Rather, she was taken from his side to complement him, near his arms to be protected by him, and close to his heart to be loved."[1] True submission never imprisons us. It liberates us, giving us the freedom to be creative under the protection of divinely appointed authority.

> True submission never imprisons us.

Most likely, before you got married
to your man's love and leadership. I
love and leadership by being thoughtful,
ing you, and bringing you gifts. You responded, .
by making yourself attractive, by seeking to please hi.
and by going places with him you may not have really
cared about simply because you enjoyed his company.
Then after your marriage, things may have changed for
the worse. What happened? Could it be that you gradually left your role of responder by no longer taking
time to look your best for your husband or refusing to
share his interests? Yes, it is easy to stop responding to
your husband without even realizing it. So many things
pull us in the opposite direction. That may include our
selfishness or lack of understanding our role in the
marriage relationship.

However, a wise woman knows that she cannot take her
role as a wife lightly. She must seriously work at building a
lasting, fulfilling relationship with her husband. *"The wise
woman builds her house, but with her own hands the foolish one
tears hers down"* (Prov. 14:1). A woman can act foolishly and
destroy her marriage, yet not be aware that she is violating
principles on which a successful marriage is built. That is
why women must be taught

> ...*to love their husbands and children, to be self-con-
> trolled and pure, to be busy at home, to be kind, and to
> be subject to their husbands, so that no one will malign
> the Word of God* (Titus 2:4-5).

Because the secular world has done an effective job
of distorting the marriage relationship and its respective
roles, many women are unfulfilled. They are convinced
that their unhappiness is caused by various factors such
as childcare responsibilities and not working outside

: home. Actually, their unhappiness may be a result of their failure to understand and fulfill the role God designed for them in marriage.

Let's go back to the illustration of the wise and foolish women mentioned in Proverbs 14:1. The wise woman recognizes God's principles for building a successful marriage and applies them. She realizes that a successful marriage requires planning, in the same way any successful venture does. For instance, in order to bake a light, delicious cake, she must put in the right ingredients at the right time, using the proper proportions. Likewise, in order to develop a happy marriage, the wise woman will use the proper principles at the right time with a divine balance. A strong marriage does not just happen accidentally. It is deliberately built through the years, through the work of both spouses.

> A successful marriage requires planning, in the same way any successful venture does.

The Old Testament book of Esther gives examples of a foolish woman and a wise woman. Foolish Queen Vashti did not respond to her husband's leadership when he requested that she join the party he was giving and allow his guests to observe her beauty. Although today we might second-guess her motives and try to justify her disobedience, she nevertheless appeared to make a foolish choice in the culture of that time. As a result, the king banished her from his presence, and he later chose Esther to be his queen.

Esther, a wise woman, responded to King Xerxes' leadership and the results were wonderful! During a period of crisis when she could have lost her life, her submissive attitude and wise actions caused the king to say, *"Now what is your petition? It will be given you. Even up to half of the kingdom, it will be granted"* (Esther 5:6). The crisis was resolved soon afterward. Esther's life and the lives of the entire Jewish nation were saved because of her right and wise actions that God blessed.

A wise woman will build a successful marriage by meeting her husband's needs as described in Proverbs 31:11-12: *"Her husband has full confidence in her....She brings him good, not harm, all the days of her life."*

I suggest that we use this verse as a measuring stick to evaluate our attitudes and actions toward our husbands. Let's each ask ourselves, *How can I comfort, encourage, and do other good things for my husband?* This may mean comforting him when his boss has made his life difficult at work or encouraging him when he begins to doubt his ability to provide financially for his family. As you act wisely, over time you will see a miraculous blossoming of your marriage relationship.

ENDNOTE

1. Matthew Henry, Commentary on Genesis 2:21-25. www.christnotes.org.

2

Your Relationship With the Designer

God created Adam perfectly and placed him in a perfect environment—the Garden of Eden. There he had fellowship with God and engaged in an interesting occupation. Yet he evidently needed a counterpart, a woman who could meet his human needs. So God provided her. *"The Lord God said, 'It is not good* [sufficient, satisfactory] *for the man to be alone. I will make a helper suitable for him'"* (Gen. 2:18). Then Adam said, *"This* [creature] *is now bone of my bones and flesh of my flesh; she shall be called 'woman,' for she was taken out of man"* (Gen. 2:23).

Because God created woman, she was perfect too. Her beauty must have been beyond anything we can imagine. Adam took one look at her and saw immediately that she was different from him, yet she was his counterpart. The New Testament echoes man's need for the woman and God's purpose in making her: *"Man did not come from woman, but woman from man; neither was man created for woman, but woman for man"* (1 Cor. 11:8-9). One beautiful aspect of God's plan through marriage is that the woman will find happiness as she meets her husband's needs. She can also tremendously influence her husband because of her special abilities to meet those needs.

The woman will find happiness
as she meets her husband's needs.

When Eve, the first woman, left her role of responding to her husband's leadership, she negatively affected all humankind (see Gen. 3:1-6, 14-19). Eve allowed satan's subtle conversation and deceit to influence her thinking and cause her to doubt that God's plan was for her good. Once she doubted God's complete love and provision, it was not long before she sinned, acting independently of God and His plan for her life.

Having made this mistake, Eve then used her influence to draw her husband into committing the same sin. *"She also gave some* [fruit of the tree of the knowledge of good and evil] *to her husband, who was with her, and he ate it"* (Gen. 3:6). She gave, and he ate! According to First Timothy 2:13-14, Adam was not deceived. He knew what he was doing. He had to choose between continuing in perfect fellowship with the Lord and joining his beloved wife in her fallen state. Knowing the consequences, he chose to live in a fallen state with Eve. Yes, the influence of a wife can be tremendous!

I'd like to get personal with you right now. If you aren't trusting God for guidance, you may be influencing your husband in wrong ways. In Genesis 16, we read that godly Sarai (later named Sarah) left her role of responding to her husband's leadership and influenced him in a sinful way. Many years had passed since God had promised them a son. Impatient, Sarai tried to help God fulfill His promise by giving Hagar, her maid, to her husband so the maid might bear them a son. In doing this, Sarai stepped out of the role God had designed for her and took matters into her own hands. So many centuries later, this sin is still causing pain for many people because the descendents of Hagar and Sarai continue to war against each other. Our role in marriage is a big responsibility as well as a wonderful privilege.

THE WOMAN'S NEED

Before she sinned (see Gen. 3), Eve was complete in spirit, soul, and body. Each day she enjoyed fellowship with the Lord and her husband. However, when she disobeyed God and ate the fruit, she died as God promised she would. She did not die physically for many years, but immediately she died spiritually. Her human spirit, the part of her that could understand God's truths and enjoy His fellowship, died. The new emptiness in her life could only be filled by regaining a personal relationship with God.

Blaise Pascal said that there is a "God-shaped vacuum" in the heart of each person that cannot be filled by anything or anyone but God, the Creator, made known through Jesus Christ.[1] Each member of the human race enters this world in the same fallen state in which Eve found herself immediately after her sin. The old sin nature has been transmitted to each of us through Adam.

> *Therefore just as sin entered the world through one man, and death through sin, and in this way death came to all men* [no one being able to stop it or to escape its power], *because all sinned* (Romans 5:12).

Each of us has a control center in our lives from the moment we come into the world. Without Christ in our lives, the old sin nature (*self, I, flesh, old nature,* or whatever term you use) is controlling us. This sin nature shows up clearly in children. We don't have to teach them to be selfish or demand their own way. They do that naturally, just as we do. The central problem in many marriages is selfishness. When we walk in the power of our carnal flesh, we can be selfish and demanding, or manipulative.

God loves you and me so much that He designed a plan whereby we could be restored to fellowship with Him without compromising His perfect character. (The barrier of sin between us and God had to be removed before God could express His love for us since His righteousness could not tolerate contact with sin. God, being perfectly just, could not overlook our sin, but required that the penalty—death—be paid.) Jesus, who is God's Son, accomplished the Father's plan by leaving the glories of Heaven in order to come to earth. He was born into the human race, adding humanity to His deity. By living a perfect life and willingly dying on the cross to pay the penalty for our sins, Jesus provided the opportunity for us to receive salvation. As the apostle Paul wrote, *"God made Him who had no sin to be sin for us, so that in Him we might become the righteousness of God"* (2 Cor. 5:21).

While Jesus hung on the cross for three hours (Matthew 27:45), the Father caused *"the iniquity of us all"* to fall on Him (Isa. 53:6). Jesus paid the full price for all our sins—past, present, and future—more than two thousand years ago. He said, *"It is finished"* (John 19:30). He did all the work necessary so we could receive salvation and enjoy an intimate relationship with Him. We cannot earn or deserve it. It is a free gift that we each must receive before it belongs to us.

Just as we could not die to pay for our own sins, neither can we live the Christian life on our own. Jesus Christ wants to relive His life in us and through us, moment by moment, if we will allow Him to do it. I love how the late Major Ian Thomas expressed this truth. He said, "I can't. You never said I could. You can, and always said you would. Behave yourself, Lord, in me."[2] Such a relationship is described in First Corinthians 1:9 and Galatians 2:20. *"…You were called into companionship and participation with His son, Jesus Christ our Lord…"* (AMP). *"I no longer live, but Christ lives in me.…"* He wants to become our companion, or inner mate, thereby fulfilling our innermost needs.[3] As we learn to live this way, in His presence, obeying the Word so that we are not deceived from the simplicity that is in Christ, we will be fulfilled (2 Cor. 3:18; 11:3). We are then able to consistently meet the needs of our husbands, for whom we were designed.

It is important that you realize all your sins have been dealt with, regardless of what they are and how great you feel they are. The issue you must face is whether you will accept or reject Jesus Christ's work for you on the cross. (See John 3:18.) There is no way to know God except through His Son. That is why Jesus said, *"I am the way and the truth and the life. No one comes to the Father, except through Me"* (John 14:6). When you accept His work on the cross for you, you become God's child.

If you're not sure that you are God's child—a member of His eternal family—why don't you make sure? The Bible says that you can know you are God's child once you have received His Son:

> *God has given us eternal life, and this life is in His Son. He who has the Son has life; he who does not have*

the Son of God does not have life. I write these things to you who believe in the name of the Son of God so that you may know that you have eternal life (1 John 5:11-13).

Right now, in the silence of your heart, you can tell the Father that you accept His perfect gift of salvation by receiving His Son as your personal Savior. You can know that you are His child on the basis of His Word, not by what you do or feel.

Maybe you have already chosen to follow Jesus. Even though you are God's child, it is possible for you to take control of your life again and feel frustrated and dissatisfied. You may experience conflicting emotions or confusion about how best to live your life. That is because the Holy Spirit is acting to guide you according to biblical principles, but your old sin nature is trying to govern your life without God's principles. Paul described it this way:

I do not understand what I do. For what I want to do I do not do, but what I hate I do. And if I do what I do not want to do, I agree that the law is good. As it is, it is no longer I myself who do it, but it is sin living in me. I know that nothing good lives in me, that is, in my sinful nature. For I have the desire to do what is good, but I cannot carry it out. For what I do is not the good I want to do; no, the evil I do not want to do—this I keep on doing. Now if I do what I do not want to do, it is no longer I who do it, but it is sin living in me that does it.

So I find this law at work: When I want to do good, evil is right there with me. For in my inner being I delight in God's law; but I see another law at work in the members of my body, waging war against the law of my mind and making me a prisoner of the law of sin at work within my members. What a wretched man I am! Who will rescue me from this body of death? Thanks be to God—through Jesus Christ our Lord... (Romans 7:15-25).

Worry, jealousy, discouragement, a critical attitude, and bitterness may be signs that you are controlling your own life. If so, recognize these symptoms as sin and claim the promise in First John 1:9: *"If we confess our sins, He* [Jesus] *is faithful and just and will forgive us our sins and purify us from all unrighteousness."*

> Worry, jealousy, discouragement, a critical attitude, and bitterness may be signs that you are controlling your own life.

When you—just now or in the past—trusted Jesus Christ to come into your life, you moved to the condition of having Jesus Christ in your life through the renewing power of the Holy Spirit, and you became a child of God. At that moment, the Holy Spirit came to live in you so you could live a Christian life (see Rom. 8:9). By faith, know that you are now indwelt and controlled by the Holy Spirit. He is now actively rebuilding your control center to act on God's Word, not the old sin nature you were born with. (See Colossians 2:6; Ephesians 5:18.)

Remember, Jesus Christ will not come into your life against your will, nor does He take control of your life without your permission. However, once you've invited Him into your life, He promises never to leave you (see Heb. 13:5).

ANOTHER KEY CHOICE

Both Christianity and marriage involve a deliberate choice. You choose to commit your total person—intellect, emotions, and will—to another. When I met DeWitt, intellectually I liked what I saw—looks, personality, and many other qualities. Yet there is more to marriage than respect and admiration. As we became better acquainted, Cupid found his mark. But our love for each other didn't make us married. We became engaged, and the wedding day arrived. Intellectually, I believed that he was the most wonderful man in the entire world. Emotionally, my heart beat twice as fast when we were together. But something more took place. When we exchanged our vows before the minister, we committed our wills to each other to fulfill our marital roles. This act of committing our entire selves—intellect, emotions, and will—to each other made us truly married.

☺ Both Christianity and marriage involve a deliberate choice.

The same is true in following Jesus. Through a deliberate commitment of our wills, each of us can become a member of God's family. Both commitments are designed to enable us to be complete, fulfilled women.

As Christ meets our personal needs, we can, in turn, meet our husbands' needs by following the pattern given in First Corinthians 7:34: *"...A married woman is concerned about the affairs of this world—how she can please her husband."* Let's begin doing the things for our husbands that we know will please them. Sew on that button he has talked about for so long. Prepare a special dinner. Enjoy a ball game or fishing trip with him. Bake the pie he loves. Go out to eat in his favorite restaurant. Train the children to remove their bicycles from the driveway. Give him a hand with a yard project or a project of his special interest. In short, make it a point to try to fulfill your husband's desires. As you do, you will find that your marriage relationship will take on new meaning.

And when things in your relationship don't go smoothly—and these times will certainly come—remember: because of Christ's victory over sin, you no longer have to panic or become upset when things go wrong. You can have control and peace through such times by drawing on Jesus' strength instead of your own. He promises to be sufficient (see 2 Cor. 9:8). Not only that, He promises to use such challenging times to shape or mold you into the image of His Son Jesus Christ (see 2 Cor. 3:18). It is as if you are a diamond in the rough being made into the image of Jesus Christ by the Master Craftsman. Each day can become an adventure if you think of its joys and trials as being part of God's process of shaping you into a divine original. You can relax, trusting His skilled craftsmanship. *"We are God's workmanship, created in Christ Jesus to do good works..."* (Eph. 2:10).

ENDNOTES

1. Pascal. Blaise. Campus Crusade for Christ, International, *The Uniqueness of Jesus* (Arrowhead Springs, San Bernardino, CA., 1964), 15.

2. Thomas, Major Ian. Personal notes taken from Major Ian Thomas' lecture in 1969 in Atlanta, GA.

3. For a detailed study on developing an intimate walk with Christ, study Darien B. Cooper, *The Beauty of Beholding God* (Shippensburg, PA: Destiny Image, 1989), which is available at www.darienbcooper.com.

3

Helping Your Husband
Love Himself

Jesus described the key to your fulfillment and contentment in Matthew 22:37-39:

> *"Love the Lord your God with all your heart and with all your soul and with all your mind." This is the first and greatest commandment. And the second is like it: "Love your neighbor as yourself."*

When the first commandment is true of your life, the second can become a reality. Furthermore, you cannot love someone else—including your husband—until you first love yourself. You can only truly love yourself when your identity is "in Him." Many of my problems have resulted when I chose to base my identity on what others said or how they treated me. When I live by the truth of what God says about me, my identity is secure. I am free to be who He designed me to be and free to love others unconditionally. You can love yourself by having your identity in Him when you see yourself from God's viewpoint.

YOU ARE ENJOYED

How awesome it is to know that your Lord not only desires to have intimate companionship with you, but that He also enjoys such fellowship. *"...You were called into companionship...with Jesus Christ our*

Lord" (1 Cor. 1:9 AMP). God also said that anyone *"...who touches you touches the apple or pupil of His eye"* (Zech. 2:8 AMP).

In another passage, God said, *"I have called you by your name; you are Mine"* (Isa. 43:1 AMP). I love the way a Bible teacher, who is more of an expert in languages than I am, explains this verse. He says that the word translated *name* can be expanded to mean "my favorite friend," one who is singled out for special honor, position, and function." *"... He will rejoice over you with joy;... He will exult over you with singing"* (Zeph. 3:17 AMP). You are His happy thought. In fact, God is always thinking about you. *"Behold, I have inscribed you on the palms of My hands; your walls are continually before Me"* (Isa. 49:16 NASB). God enjoys us even while we are still spiritually immature. What an amazing comfort and assurance!

You Have Value and Significance

You are valuable to Him, so much so that He gave His life for you. Your life was designed to have an impact for now and eternity. God assures us that this is true. *"For we are His workmanship, created in Christ Jesus for good works, which God prepared beforehand so that we would walk in them"* (Eph. 2:10 NASB).

He has personally placed you where you need to be in order to fulfill His plan (see 1 Cor. 12:11,18). And He has given you the talents and gifts you need to fulfill His plan for you (see 1 Pet. 4:10).

You Can Be a Success

When Jesus died on the cross and arose again, He made total provision for you. Read what He says:

He picked you out before the foundation of the world (see Eph. 1:4). When you said yes to Him as Savior, the deal was sealed. He promises to finish His work in you (see Phil. 1:6). You are complete in Him (see Col. 2:10). The process of completion continues while you live your life in time and space. He will meet your every need as you walk with and trust Him (see Phil. 4:19).

You are His "highly favored one." The angel Gabriel called Mary the mother of Jesus *"you who are highly favored"* in Luke 1:28. *Charitoo* is the Greek word from which this was translated.[1] This is the same word in Ephesians 1:6 translated "accepted."[2] Only two times is this word used in the New Testament. So we can accurately say that you are also a highly favored one. Mary gave birth to Jesus physically. We can birth Jesus spiritually in our lives so that others can taste of Him and want to know Him personally for themselves. Let us say with Mary, *"Behold the maidservant of the Lord! Let it be to me according to your word"* (Luke 1:38 NKJV).

Bask in these truths and begin to be firmly established in who you are in Him. Let the Spirit of God renew your mind and heal your emotions as you begin to believe you are who God says you are. As you learn to love yourself as He made you, you can genuinely love your husband and meet the needs of his life that God desires for you to meet.

Ephesians 5:33 describes one of those needs: the wife must respect. This means she notices, loves, praises, honors, and esteems him. She also defers to him when appropriate and admires his positive strengths, leaving his flaws in God's hands. Your man has a strong need to know that you are proud of him, pleased with him, and admiring of him. (If right now it's tough to do these, continue to trust God, love your husband, and focus on his strengths.) Difficult jobs become easier if he has your loving support and admiration. You see, a compliment acts as a stimulus and is a source of encouragement. A complaint, on the other hand, acts as a depressant and is a source of discouragement. I saw this truth at work when we moved to our retirement quarters. We were given the opportunity to have a new kitchen. However, it meant DeWitt would have to make the cabinets one foot shorter and skillfully fit them into our new space. He felt overwhelmed because his expertise was heavy construction not fine carpentry. Knowing this was God's gift, I encouraged DeWitt that he had successfully conquered bigger projects and I knew he could do this one also. He did and we are both regularly reminded that believing in ourselves and each other has rich reward.

As you help to fulfill your husband's need for admiration, you will help him to love himself. He, in turn, will be better able to nourish, protect, and cherish you as described in Ephesians 5:28-29:

> *In this same way* [as Christ loved the church], *husbands ought to love their wives as their own bodies. He who loves his wife loves himself. After all, no one ever hated his own body, but he feeds and cares for it, as Christ does the church.*

> As you help to fulfill your husband's need for admiration, you will help him to love himself.

Knowing that God created you and your husband to be different so you would complement each other should give you an incentive to meet his need for praise and admiration. Remember, each of you has something that the other one needs. Together you make a wonderful team. Your husband's need for admiration is fulfilled through your genuine praise. His love and strength, in turn, should meet your need for tenderness and protection. Your intuition complements his wisdom. Your loyal support undergirds his initiative. When you and your husband use these abilities to strengthen each other, you will develop a lasting marriage.

> 😊 Each of you has something that the other one needs.

You'll find further motivation to understand your role in marriage in First Corinthians 11:7: *"A man...is the image and glory of God; but the woman is the glory of man."* As your husband allows Jesus Christ to control his life by the power of the Holy Spirit, Christ's qualities will be manifested through him and he will reflect God's glory. You, however, are to reflect your husband's glory. You do this by bringing attention to his commendable qualities, praising him, honoring him, and giving him proper respect. There may be times when his behavior is not respectable. By praising his good qualities, you are not approving of his actions, but you are giving respect to his position in your life. Trust that God will use your praise to not only help your mate to know he has God-given potential, but to also draw him to walk more intimately with God.

DETECTING YOUR HUSBAND'S POSITIVE QUALITIES

As you try to sincerely praise your husband, you may need help in uncovering traits, interests, or strengths that you honestly admire. If you have a hard time finding admirable qualities in your man, believe by faith that they do exist, although they may be dormant. Remember, *"Love...always trusts, always hopes, always perseveres"* (1 Cor. 13:6-7). Discovering things about him that you may have overlooked for years will be exciting. Your unwavering belief in him will begin to reveal his positive traits. Don't push him; just believe in him, and you will begin to experience a deeper, closer relationship with your man. I have to work at not overlooking DeWitt's special strengths. He enjoys serving his family by keeping the grounds well groomed. As we were enjoying our scenic view one morning at breakfast, I said, "DeWitt thank you for all your hard work making things look so nice. I just want you to know I appreciate it and don't take it for granted." He gratefully said, "Thanks. That makes it worth it knowing that someone notices."

How do you go about detecting these hidden qualities?

Sincerely Praise Your Husband

If you want to nurture a manly man:

- ℘ Praise your husband for his physical strength and the ease with which he does manly or difficult things, such as opening tight jars, moving furniture, doing landscaping, and handling heavy equipment.

- ℘ Express appreciation when he does chores around the house instead of saying, "Well, it's about time." Your appreciation and gratitude should gradually encourage him to do things around the house if he has been unwilling to do them before. But don't be discouraged if his first reaction to your praise is a sarcastic or biting reply. He may have built a wall around himself because he's missed your appreciation in the past. Give him time.

- Compliment him on his broad shoulders, deep voice, strong hands, beard, or special, creative talents.

- Praise or show appreciation for his courage, honor, determination, cleverness, intellectual ability, achievements, skills, leadership, aspirations, or ideals. Have you thanked him lately for the hours he spends earning a living for your family? His faithfulness in providing for the family demonstrates praiseworthy qualities of dependability and responsibility.

- Praise him for the way in which he stands behind his convictions as he directs your home and household. You may not always agree with his decisions, but you can compliment him for his courage in standing by them. Approve and compliment his determination when he accomplishes his goals. You may have been calling his determination stubbornness. If you see it as a worthy trait, however, God can use you to turn it to His use. (Be sure to ask God to show you ways in which you can apply this principle of admiration to your mate's unique gifts and talents.)

These are just a few suggestions to get you started. Now I offer several words of caution:

- Start off gently, trusting Christ to point out things in your husband that you can sincerely praise. If you come on too strong at first, you may appear phony.

⊛ If you have a son, be sure to praise him for God-given qualities and traits, too. Your wisely-given encouragement will help him to develop into a stronger man, one who has a better understanding of himself and God's role for him.

⊛ Be sure that your motives are right when you offer praise. If you do it so you can change or manipulate your husband, he'll think you're flattering him or "buttering him up." Ask God to give you pure motives and then, in faith, believe that He will. When these truths were new to me and I was simply practicing the concepts to see if they worked, DeWitt regularly challenged me. For instance, if I said, "DeWitt thank you so very much for washing my car yesterday" to pave the way for asking for something I thought he might not want to do, he would respond with, "What is it you want?" Ouch! I knew I had been found out! His sharp discernment was not a comfort at the time, but it was a mighty tool in God's hand to purify my motives. I learned to praise DeWitt "as unto the Lord" rather than attempting to change or manipulate him.

LISTEN TO YOUR HUSBAND

Many of us don't know our husbands very well because we seldom quit talking long enough to listen to them. Scripture says, *"A woman should learn in quietness..."*

(1 Tim. 2:11). Even if your husband is talking about something you don't understand or feel interested in, give him your undivided attention. You'll learn a lot about him. You will begin to detect how he feels about people and situations, for example. You will even discover noble, mature dimensions in his character that you never knew were there.

DEVELOP AN INTEREST IN THINGS HE LIKES

If you are married to a sportsman, learn enough about his favorite sports or hobbies so he can talk to you about them. Perhaps you will have fun participating in some of them, too. Either way, he will enjoy teaching you some things if you show an interest.

DON'T GET DISCOURAGED

At first you may feel utterly foolish praising your husband. But if you remind yourself of his need and continue by faith to offer sincere praise, you will find that your praise comes more easily. As a matter of fact, you will probably find that you like to give sincere praise as much as he enjoys receiving it.

Many women, feeling that their husbands are already too egocentric, are afraid that if they openly express admiration, their husbands will become more boastful. Actually, the opposite will probably occur. The man who constantly brags about himself usually feels insecure and is trying to convince himself and you that he's great. "Showing off" is his attempt to bolster his ego. Give him your sincere attention and praise, and soon he will begin to believe in himself and no longer feel the need to boast. Should he be truly egocentric, your job is not to correct his weakness, but to support and encourage him in positive areas. As you pray for him, trust God to deal with his problems.

After applying these principles of admiration, a woman I met named Carol said excitedly, "I can't get over how my husband is 'eating this up!' Yesterday he stayed home for lunch about an hour and a half instead of his usual 30 minutes. I thought he would never go back to work." Laughingly, she continued. "If he keeps this up, I'll never get any work done." Of course, she was enjoying his attentiveness as much as he was relishing her admiration.

YOUR REWARD

Do you feel this marriage relationship is all one-sided, that your husband receives all the benefits? Well, cheer up. When you follow God's plan for your life, you will be rewarded fourfold. Just be careful that you do not have preconceived ideas of what that will look like. Trust God, knowing He gives us the best.

YOU'LL REDISCOVER YOUR HUSBAND

First, as you trust Jesus Christ to help you understand your husband, you will be pleasantly surprised to discover what a wonderful man you married. For the first time, you may see that he has been expressing his love for you all along. Because he did not always show it in a tender, sensitive way or the way that you would have chosen, you hadn't recognized it as love.

Perhaps he straightened up the kitchen after an argument, teased you, and built that special cabinet you've wanted, or dug up the ground by the garage so you could plant roses. Don't force your husband to express his love the way you do. Accept these loving gestures, even the teasing, as his way of saying that he loves you.

Second, as your husband begins to respond to your loving admiration, he will express appreciation and love for you. God's Word teaches that we reap what we sow (see Gal. 6:7). Your loving patience and kindness toward your husband will encourage the highest and best in him. That is worth working toward.

Every man is different, of course. One will quickly and lovingly react to his wife's overtures. Another will not react quickly or easily. It is your job to patiently respond to God and your husband in loving submission. It is God's responsibility to work in your husband's life. Trust God to repair any damage done to your marital relationship because you did not let Jesus Christ control your life. If you have sown seeds of bitterness, jealousy, or selfishness, it may take some time for God to get rid of the weeds.

Try to be honest and objective, however. Do not assume responsibilities that are your husband's alone. Realize that there are needs in his life that you cannot meet, such as his need to make Christ the Lord of his life or his need for acceptance and approval by others in business and society. Your main job is to comfort, encourage, and support your man when he is with you. As you plant and water your mate's life with praise, it is God's job to make it grow and bring an increase (see 1 Cor. 3:6-7).

God Will Give You Peace and Inner Stability

Third, God will give you inner peace and stability when you live to please and obey Him and not yourself (see Rom. 8:6-7; Gal. 5:22). If you accept your husband as he is, admire him for his positive traits and actions, and care for your household because Christ instructs you to rather than for the praise you may receive, you will not become proud when your husband praises you for your efforts. (If, for instance, you cleaned your house just to receive your husband's praise, only to have him say, "Hey, you missed that cobweb in the corner," your day would be spoiled. But if you cleaned the house first of all to please the Lord, you would not be as hurt.) Nor will you be discouraged when he fails to praise you for a job well done. You will realize that what follows as a result of your obedience to Christ is His responsibility. The apostle Paul wrote, *"He who began a good work in you will carry it on to completion until the day of Christ Jesus"* (Phil. 1:6).

You Will Receive Eternal Rewards

Fourth, you will receive rewards in eternity as you faithfully trust and obey Christ.

> *Whatever you do, do your work heartily, as for the Lord rather than for men, knowing that from the Lord you will receive the reward of the inheritance. It is the Lord Christ whom you serve* (Colossians 3:23-24 NASB).

It took this principle of eternal rewards to jolt me into confessing a sin in my life one day. I was very angry with a certain woman and was verbally tearing her apart—and enjoying it. I knew I was wrong and would lose fellowship with Christ if I didn't confess my sin. But my attitude was, "I have a few more things I want to say first." After some time, God brought the principle of eternal rewards to my mind, reminding me that my sinful attitude would cause misery for me now and that I would lose my eternal rewards (see 1 Cor. 3:11-15). That was all the reminder I needed to help me realize that I did not want to pay the high price of sin.

ENDNOTE

1. "Charitoo." Strong's Concordance, #5485
   www.bibel.def.li/Strongs/g/5450.html

4

Accepting Your Husband as He Is

The most important gift God offers us is a personal, intimate relationship with Him through Jesus Christ. His next most important gift to each of us married women is our marriages. God created and honors the marital relationship. As we respond to our husbands in the way God means us to, we can expect God to bless us.

WONDERFUL GIFT OR SURPRISE PACKAGE?

When you received the "gift" of your husband, you may have thought that he was perfect. But after the exchange of "I dos," when you began to unwrap your package, the gift turned out to be a surprise. You may have even decided that you had the wrong husband. It's important to realize that even though you did not know exactly what you were getting, God did.

One wonderful thing to remember about God is that He does not fail. If you trust Him, He will take all things and work them out for your ultimate good (see Rom. 8:28). He can use the very things in your husband that you dislike most to mold you into the image of Christ. He wants you to settle down to a lifetime of enjoying the gift you promised to honor and cherish, and learning to accept His plan for your life is vital.

WHAT ACCEPTANCE AND LOVE INVOLVE

In order to learn to love and accept others, including your husband, you must first notice how much Christ loves and accepts you: *"God demonstrates His own love for us in this: While we were still sinners, Christ died for us"* (Rom. 5:8). God loves and accepts you unconditionally. You are not on probation with Him. The apostle Paul wrote:

> *For I am convinced that neither death nor life, neither angels nor demons, neither the present nor the future, nor any powers, neither height or depth, nor anything else in all creation, will be able to separate us from the love of God that is in Christ Jesus our Lord* (Romans 8:38-39).

Unconditional love and acceptance, then, should be the foundation of your marriage, and it is vital that you give your husband these gifts. Just as a plant needs water, sun, fresh air, and room to spread its roots in order to grow and be healthy, your husband needs your unconditional love and acceptance and lots of freedom in order to love and cherish you as God meant him to. When you accept your husband the way he is, you will give him the freedom to be the man he wants (or needs) to be. In other words, true love is letting go! You will be encouraging your husband to love you freely, as he did when he chose to marry you, rather than stifling that love with possessiveness. DeWitt's forth- right frankness attracted me when we were dating. After we were married, I started taking undue responsibility for his words and actions that I thought others might misunderstand or take offense with. For instance, if he called someone stupid, I would either then or afterwards try to "straighten him out." I might say, "You never call someone stupid; it could seriously wound them." Of course all of that is true, but he needed to learn from his own actions by dealing with the person himself rather than through my interfering. Now, there were times I could offer helpful suggestions and they were received. But if my actions were stifling or possessive, it not only didn't work, but it also robbed each party from learning and growing together. What freedom it is to watch God "fix" relationships rather than take responsibility that is not mine. The Holy Spirit will help you walk that fine line or find the narrow path.

True love is beautifully described in First Corinthians 13:4-7:

> *Love is patient, love is kind. It does not envy, it does not boast, it is not proud. It is not rude, it is not self-seeking, it is not easily angered, it keeps no record of wrongs. Love does not delight in evil but rejoices with the truth. It always protects, always trust, always hopes, always perseveres.*

Remember, you do not have the power to love like that, but Jesus Christ can love through you if you allow Him to. At times, you may feel that it is asking too much of you to accept your husband as he is. But I encourage you that such actions will develop a more meaningful relationship with him because both of you will have the freedom you need to mature—as individuals and as a couple. As you love your husband unconditionally—without making unfair demands and ultimatums—you will see him drawn to you like steel to a magnet. One key for me is to remember to be vulnerable, transparent, and lovingly honest with discretion. Just this morning I said to DeWitt, "I need to apologize for making a decision for you that only you should make. When you ask if you should do a job for my sister Jan, I said no she already has that scheduled. You and she need to decide that." It turned out that he wanted to do the job and she wanted him to do it. When I get out of the middle, I see wonderful things accomplished by my Lord, and my trust in God's ways is increased.

GIVING YOUR EXPECTATIONS TO GOD

If you are like many wives I've met through the years, the root of your marital discontent and inability to accept your husband lies in your expectations of him and his failure to meet your goals. When he fails to live up to your expectations, you may be hurt, become irritated, and feel disappointed. You and your husband will only be contented and free when you quit setting unrealistic goals for him and stop expecting him to be who he is not. Allow God to conform your mate into His image rather than trying to transform him into the image you have for his life. Granted, he should meet some basic expectations such as being responsible and faithful and treating you with respect. However, imposing your preconceived ideas of how your husband should act will lead to problems, as Mary discovered.

Mary was raised in a home in which proper table manners were expected. When her new husband Don first came to the table in his undershirt and put his elbows on the table, she was shocked. As time went on, she found that he had other habits she considered uncouth. She tried to correct him, but instead of changing Don, her efforts only strained their relationship.

When Mary finally committed her expectations to God and stopped manipulating and challenging Don about his table manners, the tension between them disappeared. After that when Don came to the table properly dressed, she was grateful. When his manners didn't come up to her expectations, she noticed, but didn't allow her disappointment to surface in negative ways. And guess what? In the climate of her acceptance, Don began to choose better etiquette.

If, like Mary, you are disappointed in your husband, you may be trying to make him meet certain needs in your life that only Christ can meet. *"My soul, wait silently for God alone, for my expectation is from Him"* (Ps. 62:5 NKJV). Let your disappointment be a signal to turn to God rather than a man for your needs.

Changing Your Husband

OK, you may be thinking, *But it seems right to help my husband change attitudes, traits, and actions that are making him less attractive to me and perhaps to other people. I want him to be the best he can be.*

Be careful that your well-meaning efforts don't communicate to him, "I don't love you as you are. I want you to be different." A man wants his wife to be proud of him, not ashamed of him. When she is not, for whatever reason, he becomes discouraged. The masculine abilities God has given him to cope with life are crushed instead of liberated. He cannot live a healthy, satisfying life when he is constantly "on trial." Your intentions to change him may be sincere, but they can lead to disaster. *"There is a way that seems right to a man, but in the end it leads to death"* (Prov. 16:25).

Although you can, and sometimes should, offer suggestions to your husband, God did not give you the job of convicting him of sin and error. That is the work of the Holy Spirit (see John 16:8-11). When you take on that job, you only get in God's way and slow down His work. Neither are you to be like your husband's mother—correcting and training him. Having good intentions for his future is not enough. You must act on the principles set forth in God's Word.

> God did not give you the job
> of convicting your husband
> of sin and error.

Communication breaks down in an atmosphere of nonacceptance. When your husband tells you what he has said or done, don't just criticize, point out where he was wrong, or tell him what he should have done. If you do, he may decide it is less painful to keep his thoughts to himself and stop confiding in you. Only when he is sure of your total acceptance will he confide in you. If you hold his confidences sacred, he'll know that he can trust you not to ridicule or belittle him. If you must tell his secrets to someone, tell them to Jesus Christ.

You, the Critic

Are you aware that unasked-for advice is really veiled criticism? Yes, giving unasked-for advice is just another way of attempting to change your man.

A friend of mine, Tammy, stopped her obvious methods of correcting her husband, Jack. Yet he was not confiding in her freely, and Tammy could not understand why. One day as they were driving, he started to tell her about one of his business transactions. She began to respond in her usual way by saying, "I would have done so and so." and "Why didn't you handle it this way?"

Suddenly Jack stopped talking. When she finally got him to tell her what was wrong, he said, "You never approve or agree with anything I do. I shouldn't have tried to share this with you."

Until then, Tammy had not realized that her unasked-for advice was actually criticism of him. She honestly had not intended to put him down. Sadly, she realized that her advice or veiled criticism told Jack that she did not accept him as he was.

Let's see what Jesus had to say about criticism:

> *Don't criticize, and then you won't be criticized. For others will treat you as you treat them. And why worry about a speck in the eye of a brother when you have a board in your own? Should you say, "Friend, let me help you get that speck out of your eye," when you can't even see because of the board in your own? Hypocrite! First get rid of the board. Then you can see to help your brother* (Matthew 7:1-5 TLB).

When you criticize your husband or anyone else, you are assuming an "I'm better than you are" attitude. Wouldn't it be wiser to ask God to show you your failures and let Him deal with your husband as He sees best? Make it a habit, when you have the desire to change something about your husband, to ask Christ to show you your faults. If you follow Jesus' advice to *"be humble, thinking of others as better than yourself"* (Phil. 2:3 TLB), your critical, self-righteous, or martyr attitude will disappear.

Don't try to change your husband by demanding your way. Although you may feel that you have succeeded in some area when he gives in to your demands, he may just be trying to keep peace in the household. No permanent change will likely happen. Remember, only God changes lives; our demands do not. Over a period of time, your domineering attitude may develop coolness in your man and eventually destroy his love for you. You may win a few battles, but you will lose the war. Forfeiting a beautiful, fulfilling marital relationship is not worth the temporary "success."

Trying to change your husband by using other men as shining examples will not work, either. Refrain from pointing out the neighbor who keeps his yard well manicured when you want your husband to work in yours. If you remind him of the expensive wardrobe Bill bought Karen or about your dad's success in handling a particular situation, you are shouting loud and clear, "I am not pleased with you as you are." Manipulation won't encourage your husband to love and cherish you or to walk intimately with God.

When you do not accept your husband the way he is, he may rebel, as the writer of Proverbs suggested.

As a north wind brings rain, so a sly tongue [of a wife] *brings angry looks* [from her husband]. *Better to live on a corner of the roof than share a house with a quarrelsome wife* (Proverbs 25:23-24).

Naturally, a man rebels when a wife demands her way. He is struggling to maintain his freedom to be the man God means him to be. Rest assured that God is at work in his life, too.

You may not feel that your actions classify you as quarrelsome, although your husband has been acting angry and rebellious in return. Ask God to show you if you may unknowingly be contributing to his bad temper. If the Holy Spirit points out something wrong in your behavior, confess it as sin, and trust Him to live through you and change you. Realize that He can cause your mistakes to work together for your good as you turn to Him for guidance. God promises His children, *"I will repay you for the years the locusts have eaten...Never again will My people be shamed"* (Joel 2:25-26).

WHAT ACCEPTANCE IS NOT

Accepting your husband as he is does not mean that you approve or encourage his carnal, fleshly ways. You realize that he has choices to make just as you do. If he chooses to do what is wrong, you will separate yourself from those actions, but you will do so with humility rather than a superior attitude. For instance, if he were sharing gossip, you would not encourage such actions. Instead you might say, "I sense you feel concern because of this situation. However, since this is about our neighbors, I feel it would be more productive if you go to them directly." This can be even harder if what he is doing is also your fleshly weakness.

Accepting your husband as he is will not always mean that you like how he acts. If he has treated you badly, of course you wouldn't enjoy such behavior. While you are allowing God to heal your hurt, continue to love your husband through God's strength. The time will come, hopefully, when you will once again like your husband. Acceptance is required, but enjoyment is a blessing from God.

Acceptance also does not mean that you simply tolerate your mate. Such an attitude can produce a self-righteousness or martyr attitude in you. This attitude will not draw your mate to you or God, nor will it produce peace within you. This truth became even more real when we moved to rural north Georgia. New in the neigborhood and guests at a local church celebrating family time at the end of a vacation Bible school, I was eager to not only know the people but to make friends. This church had a sign with their beliefs posted in full view where we were gathered waiting to eat. One of their commitments was that they did not drink alcoholic beverages. So as the host asked what we would like to drink with dinner, DeWitt said loudly for all to hear, "I'll take mine 'Lite'". He was refering to the Bud Lite beer commerical. The ironry of the situation was that DeWitt's a committed non-alcoholic drinker, but this was simply his idea of humor. Since it was not the way my humor works, I longed for the floor to open up and swallow us all! You could have heard a pin drop! Finally, the conversation returned to normal for everyone except me. I did my work of forgiving DeWitt for embarrassing me and attempted to resume our relationship. I thought I was doing very well. Then God convicted me that I was simply tolerating him. I must indeed embrace who DeWitt was and let God change anything that He wanted changed. With God's grace I was able to do so. The truth is that DeWitt has been embraced by the local community in ways that I probably never will be. God's ways are simply not ours.

Iverna Thompson once said about someone she wanted God to change, "If he pleases you, God, he pleases me. If he does not please you, God, you change him."[1] I like that! I am comforted by the truth that just as God accepted me the way I am, He also loves me too much to leave me that way. The same is true for those we love.

GOD'S FORMULA FOR ACCEPTING YOUR HUSBAND

God's plan, through which you can learn to accept your husband, is clearly outlined in Philippians 4:4, 6-8:

> *Rejoice in the Lord always!...Do not be anxious about anything, but in everything, by prayer and petition, with thanksgiving, present your requests to God. And the peace of God, which transcends all understanding, will guard your hearts and your minds in Christ Jesus.... Whatever is true, whatever is noble, whatever is right, whatever is pure, whatever is lovely, whatever is admirable—if anything is excellent or praiseworthy— think about such things.*

The first step in God's plan for you and your marriage is to commit all of your problems to Him. Regardless of what has worried, upset, or irritated you, God says that you should tell Him about it. How do you commit your burdens or problems to Him? You do it by talking to Him about them. Prayer is simply opening up to Him, knowing that He understands perfectly. He will not force His solutions on you even though He is the God of the universe. Instead, He waits for you to come to Him, reveal your needs, and ask for His help.

Since God sees things from a different viewpoint and knows what's best for you, don't limit Him by telling Him when and how to answer your prayers. Let Him work out your problems according to His timing and plan. Resist the impulse to return to the problem because you've "thought of something else that might work." Trust Him to find the solution. If you don't, you're saying in effect, "God, You are not able to handle my problem."

Don't be like the woman who was walking along the road with a heavy load on her back. A neighbor stopped to give her a ride. She climbed into the neighbor's truck, but left the load on her back. "Why don't you put your load down on the truck?" the neighbor asked.

"It was so kind of you to give me a ride," she answered, "I don't want to ask you to carry my load, too."

This simple illustration reveals what you do when you do not let Jesus Christ carry all of your burdens. He died for you and paid for your sins, and He offers you victory over each problem.

After giving your problems to God and thanking Him for His faithfulness, fix your mind on whatever pure, honorable, and praiseworthy qualities your husband has (if your problem involves him). Does he get up each morning, regardless of how he feels, and go to work? Thank God. Is he kind and gentle to the children? Thank the Lord. Is he a sociable guy? Be grateful.

If you have a hard time thinking of some positive traits, think back to the qualities that drew you to him before your marriage. Those traits are still in him, but they may have been buried since then. Concentrate on his positive traits, and your focus on his weaknesses will diminish. This idea is quite different from a "self-improvement" plan because you're trusting God to improve you and your husband as you follow His guidelines for life.

At this point, it might be comforting to realize that negative traits are distorted positive traits. If negative traits can be modified or channeled in the right direction, they can become strengths. Stubbornness can become perseverance. Tactlessness can be turned to frankness. If you trust God to take care of your husband's problems and if you fix your mind on your husband's assets, you can help him turn bad traits into good ones.

Philippians 4:7 describes the results you can expect. You will experience God's peace, which is more wonderful than the human mind can understand. It is a deep, inner quietness that depends not on circumstances, but on your relationship with Jesus Christ.

The principle can be stated in this way: Problems transferred to Christ, plus focusing on the positive, equals peace.

TRY THIS!

It's time to love and accept your husband as he is. Look for opportunities to praise him rather than being critical of him. Tell him you know that you have made mistakes in responding to him and are willing to correct them. Explain that you realize you have not been as loving, understanding, and responsive as God would like you to be. Demonstrate your love through your actions as well as your words. Begin experiencing the sheer joy and freedom that comes from following God's principles! Over and over I am learning that as my motives are pure and I am vulnerable, allowing God to be my protector rather than trying to work for compliments and approval, God gives me what I need. Both DeWitt and I are then free to be ourselves and grow. For instance, after a road trip DeWitt might say, "You surely got the car dirty today. Where did you go?" My weakness would be to defend myself saying it really is not as dirty as many others who traveled that way. Then to continue my defense, I might say that I really tried to miss mud puddles. Or I might have been fleshlier saying, "If you don't want to clean my car, leave it alone but get off my case!" Such ways did not result in happy times. Now, I am learning to relax. I can agree with DeWitt saying, "Yes, it's quite a mess!" Then, DeWitt almost always says, "That's alright. I enjoy washing your car." Accepting our role and leaving the rest to God is so liberating for each of us.

ENDNOTE

1. Thompson, Iverna. via spoken recorded message.

5

Not Second Best

In order to adequately fulfill your role as a wife, you must understand the place God expects your husband to occupy in your life. According to Ephesians 5:24, the husband-wife relationship parallels Christ's relationship with the Church (all believers): *"Now as the church submits to Christ, so also wives should submit to their husbands in everything."* If you are a believer, you are to depend totally on Jesus Christ for your very existence. When you put Jesus first in your inner spiritual life, He will enable you to put your husband first in your human relationships and activities.

When your husband has the assurance that he is first in your life, his self-confidence will be strengthened; he will be better able to face the world. The fact that he may have been cut down by his business opponents or faced other difficulties will be less painful if he can return home where you accept, admire, and support him. Remember, however, that your husband needs your support, not your protection or smothering. He will develop traits of independence, courage, and confidence only as he faces and tackles his problems with your support. If you're tempted to feel sorry for him, remember that most men thrive on the challenge of caring for and protecting their families, not on being cared for and protected.

> Your husband needs your support,
> not your protection or smothering.

At the time of your marriage, you and your husband became united or "one flesh" (see Gen. 2:24). Now, no normal person will ever intentionally harm himself or herself. Yet wives often unintentionally hurt their husbands—their own flesh. As you search God's Word, study the principles in this book, and give Jesus Christ more and more freedom to control your life, He will enable you to begin to love your husband as yourself. He'll also show you ways in which you may be hurting your man unintentionally.

As you trust God to help you correct any harmful attitudes, you will become the blessing to your husband that God describes in Proverbs 18:22: *"The man who finds a wife finds a good thing; she is a blessing to him from the Lord"* (TLB). What a privilege we have to be able to meet our husbands' needs!

In light of this, let's briefly explore some attitudes and actions that keep us from being a blessing to our husbands.

ATTITUDES AND ACTIONS TO AVOID

As we study our Bibles, we will discover that these attitudes and actions are not in harmony with God's plan for us as responders:

Disloyalty

If you love your husband as yourself, you will not be disloyal. Rather, you will protect him and be loyal to him in his presence or absence. *"Love does not delight in evil but rejoices with the truth. It always protects, always trusts, always hopes, always perseveres. Love never fails..."* (1 Cor. 13:6-8).

Being loyal means that you will give up any critical attitudes you may have toward your husband and confess them as sin. Trust Jesus Christ to show you good, positive things to say about him rather than focusing on negative things. Your criticism of, or uncomplimentary attitude toward, your husband (especially in front of others) can hurt him much more than a slap in the face. Even criticism directed toward someone other than your husband may cost you his respect and trust. He will think, and no doubt justly, that your critical attitude does not stop with certain people, but influences all of your relationships.

It may help you to realize that the faults that irritate you in others are usually the ones you have trouble with yourself. That is why they irritate you. Christ said, *"Do not judge, or you too will be judged...Why do you look at the speck of sawdust in your brother's eye and pay no attention to the plank in your own eye?"* (Matt. 7:1,3). Echoing this theme, the apostle Paul wrote:

> *You, therefore, have no excuse, you who pass judgment on someone else, for at whatever point you judge the other, you are condemning yourself, because you who pass judgment do the same things* (Romans 2:1).

Selfishness

Be sure you aren't giving your husband the feeling that he rates last. After spending hours working at home and quite likely outside the home, you may think you are the epitome of unselfishness. But whose desires do you consider when you accept or reject a dinner engagement? Whose likes and dislikes do you consider when planning a meal? Whose errands do you run first? When you buy your husband something to wear, do you buy what you like or what you know he likes best? Do you plan your activities so you can visit with him after work? Remember, he can easily tell if he does not have your complete attention when he talks to you. Your uninterested look, glance at the clock, or yawn will give you away. Your interest must be sincere. Focus, with God's help, on being sensitive and responsive to his needs. Remember, as you meet the needs God designed you to meet, it can make your husband more responsive to seek God for himself.

Jealousy

If you seek to love your husband as yourself, beware of jealousy. Jealousy may communicate that you love yourself more than you love him because you want what makes you happy rather than what makes him happy. Jealousy, when your husband is doing nothing unbiblical, may simply be denying him pleasures that you think may draw him away from you. You may resent his "night out with the boys," his time-consuming career, or some other activity or person. However, if you continue to check up on your husband, you can expect strained relations with him. *"Jealousy arouses a husband's fury, and he will show no mercy when he takes revenge"* (Prov. 6:34). After urging Christians to *"live by the Spirit,"* the apostle Paul wrote, *"The acts of the sinful nature are obvious:…hatred, discord, jealousy…"* (Gal. 5:19-20). A secret of healthy living for you and your husband is found in

Proverbs 14:30, *"A relaxed attitude lengthens a man's life; jealousy rots it away"* (TLB).

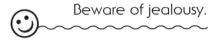
Beware of jealousy.

Yet if you love your husband as you love yourself, you will give him liberty to pursue his special interests that make him happy and are not sinful according to God's Word.

Over the years I've seen that when a man is at the center of his wife's life, he will rarely seek out another woman. Sex may not be the primary reason for a man's promiscuity. (There are exceptions when a man has developed a sexual addiction which is controlling him. He may need special counseling to overcome this.) However, often an adulterous man is looking for a woman who will accept him as he is, admire him, need him, and give him first place in her life. Yet, it's all too easy to become jealous and wonder about our husbands when we are not with them, even if they seem to treasure us. God wants to give us victory over this area from within.

"What if I lose him?" you may ask. That's a normal concern. But remember that if you are a Christian, you belong to Jesus Christ. Trust Him with your fears, and He will protect your interests. What God spoke through the prophet Hosea long ago still applies today:

> *...Then you will lie down in peace and safety, unafraid; and I will bind you to Me forever with chains of righteousness and justice and love and mercy. I will betroth you to Me in faithfulness, and love, and*

you will really know Me then as you never have before (Hosea 2:18-20 TLB).

If you ask God to take away your jealousy and trust Him to help, you will experience His peace. Yes, you and your husband will still face challenges, but God will be with you always.

I'd like to tell you about Sarah, a wife who was being consumed by jealousy—and for good reasons!

After hearing these principles about jealousy, she realized that her jealousy was one of the main factors in causing her husband to leave her, ask for a divorce, and become involved with another woman. Right away she began getting her relationship with the Lord straightened out by confessing to Him her jealousy, bitterness, resentfulness, and desire for revenge. She committed the situation to the Lord, trusting Him to look after her interests and help her to respond appropriately.

As she trusted God, moment by moment, her life began to take on a new stability, expressed through a calm and gentle spirit. During the rare occasions when her husband was home, she began to show him that she accepted him as he was, even though they both knew his actions were wrong. She found ways to express admiration for him instead of criticizing him and made the time they spent together as enjoyable as possible, given the tensions in the relationship.

Within a few weeks, he left the other woman and severed all communications with her. Shortly thereafter, he moved back home. As time passed, he began staying home all day on his day off—quite a victory. Then one day as they talked by their backyard pool, he commented, "It is just great spending time with you." This is not to imply that his infidelity did not result in deep problems that needed healing. That would be unrealistic. There had to be a defining and dealing with the facts in the situation. There is no set formula to be applied in such cases. Even if both partners cannot work through their issues together (which is ideal), the spouse that can work on personal issues should. Hopefully each will be healed in God's timing and His way. This could also include practical steps to ensure that there is no (STD)– sexually transmitted diseases.

Bossiness

Finally, don't tell your husband how to run his life. When he shares his problems with you, avoid responding to him as you might like him to respond to you. Generally, when we women have problems, we want solutions from our men. We are comforted when they either remove or solve our problems. (By the way, do not ask your husband for help with a problem unless you are ready to accept his advice or solution or at least seriously consider it.) But when your man has a problem, he probably doesn't need your solution. He probably needs you to listen, be sympathetic, and encourage him to make his own decision. In other words, you need to reinforce his faith in himself so that he will be free to use his God-given, masculine ability to face the situation and respond appropriately. If he specifically asks for your insight, lovingly share your perspective.

> Reinforce his faith in himself so that he will be free to use his God-given, masculine ability to face the situation and respond appropriately.

AREAS OF POTENTIAL IMBALANCE

When you center your activities around your husband, you will have a happy man and a balanced life. In other words, you will be the satisfied, complete woman you want to be. As you give your man his rightful place in your life, he will be more willing to give you freedom to enjoy other interests and activities as long as they don't threaten his role or position. Many men act possessive and domineering because they think that their masculine role or position in their wives' affections is not secure.

When your husband is at the hub of your activities, and the spokes (other elements) of your life are in correct proportion, the wheel (your life) will roll smoothly. If the spokes get out of adjustment, the wheel will wobble or even crash during use. The imbalance of the spokes causes the problem, not necessarily any spoke or activity itself. Let's take a look at some of the spokes of a woman's life that may tend to get out of balance and cause problems in a marriage.

Homemaking

Although a good thing in itself, homemaking can easily get out of balance and dominate a woman's life. A wife who likes to keep an immaculate house may insist, for example, that her husband remove his shoes before walking on her freshly cleaned floors. Or she may not allow him to sit on the sofa because he will mess up the cushions. Her home, rather than her husband, can assume top priority in her life. Many men resent that.

On the other hand, some women's homes look as if a cyclone has struck: Total confusion and disorder reign. This is not honoring to Jesus Christ, either. First Corinthians 14:33 reveals that God is not a God of confusion and disorder, but of peace and order. In other words, there must be a balance. Your home should be a haven, a place where both of you can relax and be yourselves. It should be a source of enjoyment and peace.

> Your home should be a haven,
> a place where both of you
> can relax and be yourselves.

Children

Children are meant to be a blessing to you and your husband. *"Children are a gift from God; they are His reward"* (Ps. 127:3 TLB).

If you put your children first, however, they will not be the joy God meant them to be. It can be so easy to center your life around them—their activities and needs—and neglect your husband. It is easy to think, *Well, he is an adult and can look after himself. My children are young and need me so desperately.* Remember, God gave the man a woman because he needed her. The relationship between you and your husband is meant to continue until death. Your children will be at home with you only a relatively short time.

Of course, you shouldn't neglect your children! When your priorities are in order, you will find that you have adequate time for both your husband and your children. Your family will be a closer unit. Your children will feel secure with parents who love each other, and your husband won't be likely to resent the children for taking his place in your life. You are free to give your best to your children when your husband is the hub of your life.

Appearance

Your appearance is another area that communicates to your husband his importance in your life. Remember, he may be exposed to stimulating, well-groomed women in the business world, and they remind him of his need for a woman. What a joy it is when he rushes home to be with you! If you work outside the home, you may already dress up. Let him know you do it for him, too! If you work in the home, obviously you won't always be dressed to go out. But try to maintain an attractive appearance, and by all means, have "dates" with your husband when you can dress up for him.

Even though you may be juggling a career, children, errands, and mountains of household work, whenever possible, arrange to spend some time with him every day, and surprise him occasionally by dressing up just for him. Your husband does not want to be taken for granted any more than you do. Give him your best whenever you can, and you will reap great dividends. When our sons were small, I set aside the last thirty minutes before DeWitt came home to straighten up the house and see that my appearance was not only acceptable but also demonstrated that I wanted to look nice for him. Having our home in order is especially important to DeWitt. A college friend of DeWitt's said before we were married, "She looks nice now, but you just wait until after you are married. That will change." My heart was and still is to see that his assessment is not true.

> Even though you may be juggling a career, children, errands, and mountains of household work, whenever possible, arrange to spend some time with him every day.

Of course you can also overdo it, spending so much time and money on yourself and your appearance that your husband may wonder if you are dressing to please him or to attract other men. Grooming can become a self-centered activity. Like other areas of your life, this one needs to be balanced.

Money and Security

It is easy to allow the area or "spoke" of money and security to dominate your life. Poor handling of money or the lack of money can be a constant source of friction between you and your husband. Because many books have been written on money management, I won't discuss the subject here except to point out that you and your husband should plan the handling of your income early in your marriage. Based on your respective skills and interests, spell out which of you will be responsible for the various money-related areas: bill paying, short-term investments, long-term investments, giving to the Lord's work, and so forth.

Interestingly, the Bible describes a happy man who is able to trust his wife in buying and selling, so it is quite biblical for a man to commit his household and money matters into his wife's hands if she is wise in these matters. Consider these verses:

> *Her husband can trust her, and she will richly satisfy his needs....She is energetic, a hard worker, and watches for bargains....She goes out to inspect a field, and buys it; with her own hands she plants a vineyard. She makes belted linen garments to sell to the merchants* (Proverbs 31:11, 16-17, 24 TLB).

When money is in short supply, your attitude toward the situation and your husband's struggle to bring in more money can make or break him. Possibly more than at any other time, your husband needs your support and encouragement. Men feel as if they've failed if they can't supply enough. Without proper support from their wives, men have turned to alcohol, other women, and even suicide during times of financial crisis. Financial problems have been attributed to 80% of marital demise according to Damon Carr.[1] Linda M. McCloud says that the number one reason for divorce is money.[2] Alison Bradbury says that financial issues are fourth in the reasons for divorce.[3] The point is that financial issues are important for a husband and wife to solve together through God's guidance. If you scold, nag, or fret, you will only increase your husband's fears and sense of failure. As you look through the situation as if it were transparent glass, seeking answers from God, this too can be a fulfillment of Romans 8:28: *"And we know that all things work together for good to those who love God, to those who are the called according to His purpose."* (NKJ). It is especially true during such times to know that God has created us for victory and through Him we can experience the good plans He has for us. See Jeremiah 29:11.

Be careful that your need for security doesn't kill your husband's incentive at work. You may resist his taking a promotion because it's a salary-plus-commission position. Perhaps you don't want to move, or you feel that your way of life will be threatened if he takes a new job. If you take that attitude, you may see your husband's interest in you, his work, and life itself begin to wane.

At the risk of seeming simplistic, I encourage you to put your trust in God rather than in your situation and finances. If you do, you'll be able to face changes in your husband's career gracefully. God warns in many Bible verses against trying to gain security from possessions. Proverbs 11:28, for example, reads, *"Whoever trusts in his riches will fall, but the righteous will thrive like a green leaf."* A man can achieve greater success financially if he is not distracted by an unfulfilled wife and if he has her support and encouragement in financial areas.

In-laws

Another area that can turn from a blessing to a curse when it's out of balance is the relationship you and your husband have with your respective parents. Problems arise when you honor your parents' wishes and desires above your husband's. The Lord addressed the in-law problem before it even existed, telling Adam and Eve, *"A man will leave his father and mother and be united to his wife, and they will become one flesh"* (Gen. 2:24).

Once you and your husband become one flesh in marriage, your husband—not your parents—are to be the center of your life. Do not make your husband feel that he must compete with your parents—or with his. When he knows he is first in your life, he will appreciate the parents who gave him such a wonderful wife. Of course, you are to continue to honor and respect your parents and his. Call or write them occasionally and share some bit of family news, such as a child's good report card, a cute thing a child has said or done, or your husband's promotion. *"Honor your father and mother'—which is the first commandment with a promise—that it may go well with you and that you may enjoy long life on the earth"* (Eph. 6:2-3). You can benefit from their maturity and experience as they give you words of counsel. This area was not hard for DeWitt and me when it came to leaving and cleaving. We moved to another state after we married where we knew no one else. In a way this helped us to completely depend upon each other. Means of communication was not as convenient as it is today. Even though we visited our families quite often, we knew this was our time to be independent and self-reliant. Once when there was a conflict about taking a parent's advice, we took a unified stand for what we knew was right. We seek to give our children the same freedom.

Outside Activities

The last "spoke" I'll discuss is that of outside activities: your social life, church work, business-related activities, clubs, and so forth. "Surely my husband knows he is more important than my outside interests," you may say. But how is he to know that? He must judge by what he sees and hears. If you spend most of your time directing the women's group at church or a Girl Scout troop, what conclusion can he reach other than that those activities are more important to you than he is?

Even though many activities are beneficial, they can take up so much of your time and attention that your husband may feel that he is less important to you than they are. In fact, if your husband is not a Christian and you talk too much about Jesus Christ, read your Bible in front of him all the time, or always go to church meetings, your husband could even begin to feel about Christ the same way he would feel about a man with whom you were having an affair. This may sound ridiculous, but perhaps all he knows is that someone else has priority in your life.

If your husband is not a Christian, he does not grasp spiritual truths.

> *The man who isn't a Christian can't understand and can't accept these thoughts from God which the Holy Spirit teaches us. They sound foolish to him, because only those who have the Holy Spirit within them can understand what the Holy Spirit means. Others just can't take it in* (1 Corinthians 2:14 TLB).

A Christian husband can also be "turned off" to spiritual truth by an overenthusiastic Christian wife who constantly talks about spiritual truths she has just discovered, especially if he is not equally interested.

You will guide your husband toward spiritual values by incorporating them into your life, thereby becoming the wife he wants you to be.

> *Wives...be submissive to your husbands that if any of them do not believe the word* [of God], *they may be won over without words but by the* [godly] *behavior of their wives, when they see the purity and reverence of your lives* (1 Peter 3:1-2).

This does not mean living by some group's "dos or don'ts," however.

Suppose a woman and her husband are enjoying certain activities together when suddenly she becomes a Christian and starts changing her way of life. He finds himself spending time alone because she is either at church or refuses to go certain places with him that they once enjoyed together. Her husband may feel threatened by the sudden changes in her because he sees their relationship being destroyed. Jesus can give the wife wisdom in loving her husband where he is.

THE IMPACT OF YOUR FAITH ON YOUR HUSBAND

Usually, as a woman trusts Jesus Christ, her life will demonstrate stability and inner happiness that will help draw her husband toward Christ. But not always. *"For how do you know, O wife, whether you will save your husband? Or how do you know, O husband, whether you will save your wife?"* (1 Cor. 7:16 NASB).

God's heart is to give us the best, purest marital relationship possible. What did Jesus mean by the following verses that may seem harsh on the surface?

> *Do not think that I have come to bring peace upon the earth; I have not come to bring peace but a sword.... If anyone comes to Me and does not hate his [own] father and mother [in the sense of indifference to or relative disregard for them in comparison with his attitude toward God] and [likewise] his wife and children and brothers and sisters—[yes] and even his own life also—he cannot be My disciple* (Matthew 10:34; Luke 14:26 AMP).

What God calls us to hate is the continuing carnal influence, fleshly ties, and loyalties that keep us from giving Him first place in our lives. He wants us to draw our strength first of all from God, not from others or others from us. Then we can be appropriately dependent on our husbands and at the same time properly independent. His word cuts away everything that is destructive for our purification. This is true love. It releases us to be all that He's designed us to be. Division in the home comes from sin in the life of the husband or wife, not from God.

Regardless of your husband's spiritual status, your role—your way of relating to him—should be the same. If he is a Christian, or when he becomes one, you will share spiritual truths together as he takes the lead or God leads you to share. Generally speaking, spiritual truths you learn are for your edification, not for you to teach to your husband. When you have the strong desire to share these truths without your husband's encouragement, pray for him instead.

> Regardless of your husband's spiritual status,
> your role—your way of relating to him—
> should be the same.

Margaret applied these principles in her marriage. When James, her husband, asked how she had become such a wonderful wife, she gently explained, "Jesus Christ is the source of my inner peace; He gives me the power to be the wife I should be." By responding to her husband as she did, Margaret did not make him feel that she no longer needed him. Christ had enabled her to willingly be dependent on her husband in their marital relationship.

Place Your Husband at the Center of Your Life

Now that you've read this far, do you feel that making your husband the true center of your life is too big an order for you to fill? I hope so, because then you will see your need to let Jesus Christ take over and help you do it. Your order is not too big for Him to fill. He is the only one who can make you the real woman you want to be. *"...A wise, understanding and prudent wife is from the Lord"* (Prov. 19:14 AMP).

Jesus Christ uses the laboratory of marriage to make us godly women. After all, marriage reveals who we really are. It brings out our habits, for example, and exposes our strengths and weaknesses. Our husbands do not make us what we are; they simply act as a stimulus to bring out what is on the inside. That's why God cautions each of us, *"Above all, guard your heart, for it is the wellspring of life"* (Prov. 4:23).

> Our husbands do not make us what we are; they simply act as a stimulus to bring out what is on the inside.

Even we Christians will have our sin nature until we die and are with Christ, but we do not have to be under sin's control. If Jesus Christ is the source of power in our lives, He will enable us to form new response patterns to life situations—including our marriages. We do not need to be slaves to the sin nature. God will enable us to break its hold on us—including its habitual patterns—so we can live according to the Spirit (see

Rom. 8:1-4). Each time we feel the pull of the sin nature as it tries to control us, we can simply turn to God and ask for His deliverance from the temptation to respond in old sinful patterns.

Temptation or evil thoughts are not sin. It is what we do with them that determines whether they become sin. The apostle James wrote:

Each one is tempted when, by his [or her] own evil desire, he is dragged away and enticed. Then, after desire has conceived, it gives birth to sin; and sin, when it is full-grown, gives birth to death (James 1:14-15).

Our freedom to choose is similar to a CD player filled with several disks. We may play the CD of old habit patterns formed by the sin nature. Or, we may skip that CD and move to the new CD of life in the Spirit. The choice is ours. If we trust Christ to control us fully and give Him the freedom to do His wonderful, life-changing work in all areas of our lives, we will begin to fall into line with God's plan for us. When Christ is first in our inner spiritual life, He will help us to put our husbands first in our human relationships and activities because that is His plan for us as wives.

ENDNOTES

1. Carr, Damon. From article, "Until "Debt" Do Us Part." Internet.

2. McCloud, Linda M. From article, "Top Reasons People Divorce." Published June 01, 2006. She is a featured health & wellness contributor; also featured dieting & weight loss contributor. Internet.

3. Bradbury, Alison. From article, "The Top 5 Reasons for Divorce." Alsion is a legal specialist and writer for http//www.divorceguide.com. Internet.

6

Follow the Leader

In any successfully functioning unit, someone must assume major responsibilities, make final decisions, and direct activities in order to prevent disorder and chaos. Yet frequently families ignore this principle of leadership and, therefore, do not experience the harmony and peace God desires them to enjoy. Since the family is the basic unit of society, its stability will determine not only the security and happiness of its members, but also the strength of our nation. Stability for the home and nation depends on our recognition of our husbands as the leaders of our families. If you find this principle difficult to grasp or it even makes you a bit angry, please keep reading.

> In any successfully functioning unit, someone must assume major responsibilities, make final decisions, and direct activities in order to prevent disorder and chaos.

If you are like many women today, your reaction will be like my own first reaction to God's plan for our husbands to be the head of the home—rebellion. Before I understood that God's plan was for my benefit, I rebelled against the thought of being subject to my husband, yet his equal.

THE DIVINE ORDER

God designated the man as the undisputed head of the family when He said to Eve, *"...Your desire will be for your husband, and he will rule over you"* (Gen. 3:16). This same principle is reaffirmed in the New Testament in Ephesians 5:22-23:

> *You wives must submit to your husbands' leadership in the same way you submit to the Lord. For a husband is in charge of his wife in the same way Christ is in charge of His body the church. (He gave His very life to take care of it and be its Savior!)* (TLB).

Society did not assign this position of leadership to man; he was divinely appointed to be the "head of the family." God's order for the home is that the husband be the head of the wife as Christ is the head of the Church and the head of man. *"The head of every man is Christ, and the head of the woman is man, and the head of Christ is God"* (1 Cor. 11:3). Through this divine order of authority, God is able to deal directly with both the man and the woman, providing them each with total fulfillment.

Remember, our position in God's divine order has nothing to do with our individual worth or importance. In Galatians 3:28, we read, *"There is neither Jew nor Greek, slave nor free, male nor female, for you are all one in Christ Jesus."* A wife tends to differ from her husband in her interests, thinking, and abilities, as well as obvious physical differences. These distinctions make her the husband's complement, but they do not make her inferior. Neither man nor woman has cause for boasting. Neither needs to fret about having an inferior position.

A home with two heads, or one in which the wife is the head, has distorted the order of the man's and woman's roles, thereby creating an abnormal condition. God designed the home to run efficiently with the man as the leader. Ignoring this principle of his leadership or devising substitutes has created untold problems. I have observed over the years that forsaking God's order for the home has contributed to the rise in juvenile delinquency and rebellion, the divorce rate, and the number of frustrated women.[1] When wives leave their position of responder and get between their husbands and God in a position of leadership, the fulfillment they are designed to receive from their marital role is diminished.

God the Father designed, for our benefit, this order of authority that can be described as "God's umbrella of protection."[2] Let's explore God's order together.

- God the Father—forms the large shield of protection over all creation

- Christ—though equal to God, places Himself under God's umbrella and is, Himself, an umbrella of protection for men charged with family and work responsibilities

- Man—covered by the direct protection of Christ, is charged with providing a covering of protection for his wife and children

- Woman—is under the protection of her husband

- Children—are under direct protection of their parents.

Christ, who is God and equal with the Father, is subject to the Father. Likewise, the man is subject to those in authority over him: God, and others such as government officials and employers (although all men are equals). The wife is subject to her husband, although she is his equal. The children are subject to their parents' authority, although they are not inferior. God uses this order of authority to protect us and provide us with maximum happiness.

The woman, operating under God's prescribed umbrella of protection for her, assumes her role of supporting and encouraging her husband and caring for her home and children. As she responds to her husband's leadership, she enjoys protection and fulfillment in the position that God designed for her. She does not assume pressures and problems that might be draining on her. She also has the freedom to participate in activities that do not conflict with her role of wife and mother, which may include working outside the home, serving as a volunteer, and so forth. Many wives have discovered ways to juggle home and career while maintaining strong relationships with their husbands and children. If a wife does work fulltime outside the home, the responsibilities of the home should be shared. When this book was first released, I was teaching this material biweekly to two different groups in the spring and fall in metropolitan Atlanta. Pastors started calling from other areas asking that I do a conference in their churches. When I asked DeWitt for his advice, he said, "Yes, I think you are to do this. But you should reduce your teaching load in Atlanta and not travel more than once a month." I also had peace about that and soon had a full schedule. However, I never left town without the house clean, clothes clean, meals prepared, and their blessing. After two years I began to notice that DeWitt was not quite as enthusiastic when he took me to the airport. I also noticed that our younger son seemed to resent my being so busy. Thirdly, my energy was not as full as it had been. As I sought God for His direction, He showed me that I was in danger of not being what I believed and was teaching. His plan was to expand my ministry by making the truths transferable through various teaching aids and allowing others to teach. This not only expanded my ministry and gave me more time to write other books, but it also gave me more time with our sons as I worked from home. Each family is unique. If you work outside the home, ask God for creative ways to share the workload. He may show you how to make the family responsibilities not only a fun family time but also a training time for the children. If your husband is resistant, choose a time to talk with him about this when you are calm and free of distractions, and not in the middle of a fight. Appeal to your partner's sense of fair play. Communicate clearly and work with him to create a united, planned approach to getting chores done. Above all, watch for ways God may be creatively guiding your family.

Under God's umbrella of protection, the husband's sphere of responsibility includes his leadership in the home as well as his responsibilities in business and society. Through his position, he has the opportunity to develop his masculine, God-given strengths and abilities.

When you are having doubts as to how to respond to your husband, remember that the husband-wife relationship is an earthly picture of the relationship between Christ and the Church (believers). Just as Christ is the head of the Church, so husbands are the heads of their wives. In this atmosphere, you are protected and fulfilled, your husband is inspired to be the man God created him to be, and your children are provided with an ideal atmosphere in which to develop and mature. God's plan is all-inclusive—total provision for everyone.(Many may find themselves single for various reasons. Allow Jesus to be your Husband walking intimately with Him. Consider wise counsel from parents, pastor, or other godly men as well as role models for your children.) You are to be totally surrounded by His loving protection—His umbrella (divine order) above and His loving hand underneath. *"Though he* [the righteous] *fall, he shall not be utterly cast down, for the Lord grasps his hand in support and upholds him"* (Ps. 37:24 AMP).

If you still have feelings of anger and rebellion when you consider your husband being the head of the home, I understand. Read prayerfully once again the description of God's umbrella of protection earlier in the chapter as well as meditating upon the diagram in Appendix A as you trust God to give you His perspective. When you look to your husband for direction, see through him as if he were transparent glass. Realize it is really God whom you are trusting. Your husband is not perfect, just as you are not perfect. But you can trust the Perfect One. Everything your husband says or does may not be God, but with God's help, you can *"take out the precious from the vile"* (Jer. 15:19 NKJV) and hear what God is saying. Should you need counsel in untangling the precious from the vile because of your emotional involvement, call your pastor or a godly counselor. God's umbrella of protection is for our blessing and protection, as Romans 13:1-5 points out. To remove yourself from that covering in rebellion or anger makes you open to the enemy's attacks, according to Ephesians 4:26-27.

ROLES OF THE HUSBAND AND WIFE

Some people think marriage is a 50-50 deal, but it is not. It requires 100 percent from each partner. You and your husband each have a role that demands your all. Each role, equal in importance to the other, carries with it different responses and responsibilities. The fact that the roles are different does not mean that one is inferior to the other. Each role is judged in terms of its function and cannot operate efficiently without the other. You and your husband complement each other in much the same way as a lock and key go together. Either is incomplete without the other.

> Some people think marriage is a 50-50 deal, but it is not. It requires 100 percent from each partner.

The roles of the husband and wife could be compared to the president and vice president of an organization. Each of them, having accepted their positions, understands that their respective positions carry heavy responsibilities. Since the structure is clearly established, there is never any doubt about who is the president. However, the president's success depends on the vice president's help. When decisions have to be made, the president may consult the vice president, but he assumes responsibility for the final decision.

Once a decision is made, both leaders work together as a team to implement it. The president may delegate authority to the vice president. When the president is traveling, he can trust the vice president to carry on as if he were there. In this relationship, they share a oneness, good communication, emotional peace, and security (provided the vice president is not struggling to gain control of the organization).

Yet, God meant the husbands and wives roles to be different. After all, he made them male and female (see Gen. 1:27), not genderless. These differences are not only physical, but are also emotional and temperamental. Although I recognize the dangers of stereotypes and overly general statements, I'll share some basic differences. Typically, masculine traits include the ability to see the overall picture in a situation and to be firm and decisive when solving problems. Feminine traits typically include the ability to see the details of a situation and to contribute valuable insights based on a compassionate, sensitive nature. For instance, as you prepare for a business party in your home, you may be caught up in the details of the preparation or how to prevent Mrs. X from offending Mrs. Y. Your husband may be thinking in terms of how the party may contribute to his business success during the coming year. By using your respective natural traits, you will be able to work together as a team.

If you do not recognize that God designed you and your husband to complement each other, you may try to force your husband to act and respond to various situations as you do. If you succeed, he will have to switch to the feminine role of being the responder, abandoning some of his masculine responsibilities. If you recognize, however, that by nature your roles are different, you can develop your feminine traits and have an even more vital role in your marriage and other areas of interest and responsibility.

Learning about our roles and their descriptions is good. However, we must remember that our identity and worth is in God, not our assignment. What if our Lord would rearrange our tasks? Would this be a problem? If so, our identity may have inadvertently been switched to what we do rather than who we are in Him. That must never happen. According to the season of our life, we can do different tasks. For instance, when our sons were small, I longed for a maid to do my housework. The Lord lovingly said, "You learn your greatest truths on your knees cleaning the bathroom!" Now that DeWitt is retired, he has faithfully cleaned our home and even makes our bed shortly after I get up. I now have a live-in maid! I am blessed that he is mutually submissive by being willing to do whatever needs to be done without ascribing certain chores to his gender.

DOES MY ADVICE OR OPINION COUNT?

Your advice and insights are valuable assets to your husband. To maximize their effectiveness, consider the following suggestions.

Your husband will value your advice more highly if he asks for it, which he probably will if you are being loving and kind. When he asks your opinion, answer him objectively, sticking to the issue and the facts involved. Remember, men tend to use speech to express ideas and communicate factual information, while women have a tendency to use speech to express feelings or vent their emotions. As you give your opinion, try not to overly express your emotions. Briefly share, on the basis of facts, your perspective of the situation. (If needed, you may allow a godly confidant, or better yet your Lord, to help you sort through your emotions before sharing with your mate if he tends to not be patient with your doing so with him.)

You may be thinking, *Do I have to wait until I am asked to share my opinion?* Only if you know your husband does not want unasked-for advice. Your judgment, wisdom, and opinion—given in love—are great assets to your husband. To withhold these insights would be a great injustice. Being submissive does not mean saying nothing; it means putting yourself completely at the service of the person who is over you.

Many times your husband needs insights or information in order to make wise decisions or to formulate correct viewpoints. For instance, if you have children, you are probably more closely involved with your children's activities and friends than your husband. To aid him in making decisions and establishing policies regarding the children and their activities, you may need to contribute information. Also, you may be able to share insights based on God's Word that will help him to avoid or correct a wrong and destructive viewpoint. Describing a wife of noble character, the wise man wrote, *"Her husband has full confidence in her....She speaks with wisdom..."* (Prov. 31:11,26).

The Bible gives a powerful example of a wife who helped her husband to correct his point of view. Manoah and his wife had no children. The angel of the Lord appeared to her and told her that she would bear a son, Samson, who would begin to rescue Israel from the Philistines.

After his wife told Manoah about the angel's visit, he prayed that God would send the angel again to give them more instructions about bringing up the boy. When the angel of the Lord returned, Manoah did not recognize him until the angel ascended into Heaven.

"We are doomed to die," he said to his wife. "We have seen God!" But his [sensible] *wife said to him, "If the Lord had meant to kill us, he would not have accepted a burnt offering and grain offering from our hands, nor shown us all these things or now told us this"* (Judges 13:22-23).

You can be a great help to your husband by sharing your insights in the proper way. True, it is best that you give him advice in a feminine manner as described in Proverbs 31:26, speaking with wisdom and having *"faithful instruction"* to share.

Ask yourself, *How will my words or actions affect my husband? Will what I say or do in a certain situation jeopardize his position as my leader?* If you consider these questions before you speak or act, you will be more apt to obey the "law of kindness" and will not run the risk of undermining his role as leader.

Never attempt to force your point of view on your husband. Simply say, "I feel this way," or "I believe such and such." Leave him free to use or not use your advice as he sees best. Your job is to enhance his role as leader, so don't give advice on a man-to-man basis or with an attitude of authority, superiority, or motherliness. Express your thoughts lovingly, leaving the final decision to your husband, assuring him of your support.

If you believe he is making the wrong decision, however, you may appeal your case to a higher court (pray about the situation and trust Christ for the ultimate outcome). Contributing your advice in this way will relieve you of the burdensome responsibility of the final decision and will support and encourage your husband.

ENDNOTES

1. Statistics vary from source and seasons. Yet Galatians 6:7-9 reminds us if we do not live by the Spirit we will reap the fruits of the flesh. Forsaking God's Word and plan leads to unpleasant results. If this does not change, the results are heartbreaking.

2. See Appendix A for a drawing of God's Umbrella of Protection of the Divine Order.

7

Protection for Your Benefit

Under God's umbrella of protection, as we explored in the last chapter, your husband is to be God's earthly agent through whom God protects you physically, psychologically, and spiritually. God's provision is complete. He planned for your husband to stand between you and the world in order to protect you from harmful physical, emotional, and spiritual pressures, which he was designed to carry. As you allow your husband to carry out this privilege, you will begin to experience the pleasure and benefits of being feminine.

PROVIDING PHYSICAL PROTECTION

In what way do you need physical protection? You may need protection from laborious tasks as well as from physical attack. Let's face it! Most likely you are not as strong physically as a man. Peter wrote, *"Husbands,...be considerate as you live with your wives, and treat them with respect as the* [physically] *weaker partner..."* (1 Pet. 3:7). Your husband may need to protect you from such hard tasks as moving a piano, pulling out an automobile engine, or carrying bundles of shingles. If you enjoy such activities, there is no condemnation, guilt, or stereotyping. Simply evaluate how this affects your mate or your physical health. You also may need protection from physical or sexual attack, even though you may have taken classes in self-defense.

Sometimes your husband may need to protect your health by encouraging you to curtail your activities. If he has complained about your busy schedule, he may be worried about you. He may be expressing his love by saying that your health is important to him. Thank him for his concern and let his advice be a reminder that you may be doing more than God planned for you to do.

Your husband also protects you physically by providing some or all of your food, clothing, and shelter. God gave him this obligation: *"If anyone does not provide for his relatives, and especially for his immediate family, he has denied the faith and is worse than an unbeliever"* (1 Tim. 5:8). Notice that God gave this warning to the man, not to the woman.

Your husband's work is a blessing.

Your husband's work is a blessing. It provides him with the opportunity to develop his God-given abilities as he faces struggles, burdens, and difficulties on behalf of his family. Be careful not to deny your husband the respect, honor, and deep satisfaction of fulfilling this role God assigned him. We read in First Thessalonians 4:11-12:

> *Make it your ambition to lead a quiet life, to mind your own business and to work with your hands, just as we told you, so that your daily life may win the respect of outsiders and so that you will not be dependent on anybody.*

Even as it is primarily your husband's job to provide the money for your family's needs, so it is your responsibility to support—and give wise input to—the financial plans. You should willingly make any effort necessary to stretch the dollars, as described in Proverbs 31:13-14. *"She selects wool and flax and works with eager hands. She is like the merchant ships, bringing her food from afar."* There are many ways to make the dollars stretch—finding bargains, cooking economical dishes, learning to sew, and so many other ideas God will give you. Many great books have been written for people who want to use their money wisely.

> As you limit your lifestyle to the money that comes in, God will direct your family finances.

As you limit your lifestyle to the money that comes in, God will direct your family finances. He will provide for you in ways that will not cause your husband to feel inferior if, for some reason, he can't earn enough. God may lead a neighbor to give you the piece of furniture you need or an aunt to mail you the special dress you prayed for. Too often, by using credit cards, you can limit God and place your family under unnecessary financial strain.

Be careful never to belittle your husband's producing power. Such comments as "We can't afford this," or "I have to skimp and save to make ends meet," will discourage him. Try not to comment too much on the ways in which you have economized in order to help out. Thriftiness is good and will give you a feeling of satisfaction, but telling your husband about it may only remind him that it is necessary because of his limited income. Help your husband in his role of being the main financial protector by your quiet economy, open support, and gratitude for his provision for the family. God knows what you and your husband need financially, so His answers to your prayers will fulfill your current needs.

If an emergency arises, such as your husband becoming ill or losing his job, you may be forced to become the primary financial provider. Proverbs 31:24 describes the working woman: *"She makes linen garments and sells them, and supplies the merchants with sashes."* You can help out financially without harming your husband if you don't give the impression that you are a martyr or a rescuing hero.

In some circumstances, you may find that outside work is advisable for you. If you have no children, or if they are now grown, a job that does not interfere in any way with your role as a wife may be just the thing for you. Working under these circumstances, or as I do in writing and lecturing, should be an avocation rather than to supply most of your family's income.

Here are a few questions to help you determine if your income-generating activity is healthy for your marriage:

1. Does your activity conflict or compete with your husband's schedule or your duties as a wife and/or mother?

2. Does your husband feel your activity is more important to you than he is?

3. Does your activity break the team unity you have as a couple?

4. Does your husband still feel responsible for providing for his family?

PROVIDING PSYCHOLOGICAL
PROTECTION

Threats to you do not stop at the physical level. You may also need psychological protection. Your emotions are a wonderful part of your femininity when they express themselves in loving response, appreciation, warmth, or kindness. But when you assume responsibilities that belong to your husband, you may encounter situations that subject you to undue emotional pressure. Your emotional responses could then to be ones of anger, frustration, and hurt. You may mishandle situations because you are so upset, and you may end up behaving like a shrew. This is often the case when you must deal with offensive salesmen, belligerent creditors, irritable neighbors, or even your inconsiderate teenagers. Your husband can then serve as a protective buffer between you and such pressures. So the next time your neighbor complains about your crabgrass getting into his lawn of fescue, simply say, "I'll speak to my husband about it." It's his problem, not yours. Isn't that comforting to stay within our God-given roles, allowing Him to use the pressures in the proper way that He so designed for growth and maturity in each of us?

As you fulfill your role, you can expect your husband to protect (or to begin to learn to do so) you from emotional conflicts in other areas, too. For example, he should lead your children to respect you and treat you accordingly. He should also carry the major responsibility in the financial worries. When you do not understand that finances are primarily your husband's responsibility, you may become emotionally upset about how the bills will be paid. Most likely your husband has the capacity to cope with this pressure. Of course you should be understanding and cooperative, but watch this area carefully. If your husband has given you the job of paying the bills, keep him up to date on family finances. But if you are handling the finances in order to control the "purse strings," you are trying to lead. You're usurping your husband's role and may open a leak in God's umbrella of protection.

PROVIDING SPIRITUAL PROTECTION

Most wives are usually least aware of their need for protection in the spiritual realm. Yet this is one of our more vulnerable areas. Being more emotional, we may be deceived into making decisions on the basis of what appeals to us or what appears to be right instead of making decisions based on objective principles set forth in God's Word.

Eve made her decision to eat the forbidden fruit in the Garden of Eden, for instance, on the basis of emotional appeal, and you know the consequences! *"Adam was not the one deceived; it was the woman who was deceived and became a sinner"* (1 Tim. 2:14). If you and I do not regulate our lives by God's Word, we will be easily led astray, too. How well the psalmist understood this: *"I have hidden Your word in my heart that I might not sin against You"* (Ps. 119:11).

It should be comforting to know that God can, literally, show us His will for our lives through our husbands. If you have prayed about a certain matter, for example, and feel that you know God's will, use God's final check. Ask your husband what he is seeing. He may say no to what you feel God wants you to do, but God can change your husband's mind if that is what is needed. The Bible says, *"The king's heart is in the hand of the Lord, as the rivers of water; He directs it like a watercourse wherever He pleases"* (Prov. 21:1). If God can change a king's mind at will, can't He also cause your husband to go along with something that is in God's plan for you?

You can trust God to lead you and your family spiritually without having to defy your husband. Otherwise, if you get out from under God's umbrella of protection and become the spiritual leader in your home at the expense of your husband's headship, everyone will suffer. After God told Rebekah that Jacob would be the master over Esau (see Gen. 25:23), she still did not trust God to work things out His way. So she conspired with her favorite son, Jacob, to deceive her aged and blind husband, Isaac (see Gen. 27). Through her deception, Jacob received his twin brother Esau's patriarchal blessing, but much heartache resulted. Esau's murderous hatred banished Jacob from his home for more than 20 toil-filled years, and Rebekah died without seeing Jacob again. It seems logical to conclude that her deceit also put a wedge between her and Isaac.

Through the years, as I explored the husband's role in providing spiritual protection for his wife, I discovered that my attitude toward my husband revealed my spiritual condition. I was rebellious to Christ's leadership to the same degree that I rebelled against my husband's leadership.

Let's look at a real-life example. Sue had trouble accepting this principle until Christ made it obvious one day. She was working in her flower garden when her husband asked her to empty the garbage can. *Why should I stop what I'm doing to do that?* she thought rebelliously. *I'll do it later, but not now.* A day or two afterward, the Holy

Spirit prompted Sue to share with her neighbor how she might know Christ personally. Sue's immediate response was, *Lord, I'll do it later, but not now.* Yes, her response to Christ was identical to her previous response to her husband—the one whom God had put in authority over her. God is faithful to expose the thoughts and intents of our hearts when we desire to know and do His will.

How to Help Your Husband Become the Leader

Sure, I'm convinced that my husband should be the head of our home, you may be thinking, *but he simply is not a leader.* Remember, though, God would not command the man in Ephesians 5:23 to be the leader (*"The husband is the head of the wife as Christ is the head of the church..."*) without giving him the ability. With God's help and yours, your husband can be the leader God means for him to be.

> With God's help and yours, your husband can be the leader God means for him to be.

If you have willingly or unwillingly assumed the role of leadership in your home, begin to ease out of it by gradually transferring to your husband the responsibilities he will most easily accept. When you begin to tell the children, "Go ask Daddy; he is the head of our home," they may be as shocked as their father, but this is a good way to start. When your display of confidence in his leadership convinces him that his leadership is a permanent arrangement, not a temporary "kick" of yours, he should begin to respond positively. He likely will enjoy the ego-boosting experience of taking charge and having you and the children follow his advice or decisions. He'll gradually gain confidence in himself and enjoy his new role.

Of course, you may have reservations about your husband's leadership. "What happens when he makes the wrong decisions?" you may ask. Well, just remember that in trusting your husband, you are actually trusting Jesus Christ. He has promised to direct you through your husband. He can even use your husband's mistakes to teach him—and you—valuable lessons if you stay under the "umbrella" of His protection. Remember Romans 8:28 says, *"In all things God works for the good of those who love Him...."*

Suppose your husband must make an important business decision and asks for your advice. You warn against the venture, but he overrules your recommendation and goes ahead. As you predicted, the decision is a mistake. You now have the choice to either ruin God's teaching opportunity by saying, "I told you so" or to maintain a sweet, understanding attitude. If you have the proper attitude in this situation, you both can benefit from his mistake. You may learn, for instance, that you have been putting your trust in money rather than turning to Christ for your security. As you maintain a gracious attitude and trust God, He will be able to deal with your husband directly and will not have to work against the interference of a nagging wife.

This promise applies to you and your husband. As you make mistakes (and you will), pray that God will work them out to glorify Him. I used to have a button on my dressing table that comforted me. It has these letters on it—PBPGINFWMY—which stand for "please be patient, God is not finished with me yet." Only God can turn our mistakes into blessings as He makes us more like Jesus.

Let go! Relax. You can enjoy the freedom of knowing that, along with the right to make the final decisions, your husband carries the responsibility for the consequences of his decisions. Resist temptations to interfere with his leadership because you feel he has not made the decisions or taken the actions you would have. Don't argue your point or try to manipulate him. Respond to his leadership in a relaxed manner, and you will find that your husband usually will want to please you.

LEADERSHIP FRUITS

Each year when they traded in their car, Peggy and Ken debated about whether they would buy the small car Ken wanted or the larger one Peggy wanted. Her persistence usually won out. After learning the principle of how to give advice, though, she simply shared with Ken her desire for a larger car—without arguing or manipulating—and left the final decision with him. She decided to trust God regardless of the outcome, so you can imagine her surprise when he returned with the larger car!

I don't mean to imply that you will always get your way. Karen wanted very much to go to a Sunday school party, but her husband decided they would stay home and watch a football game on TV. As it turned out, Karen discovered a greater joy in committing her disappointment to Christ and watching the football game with Joe than she would have received if she had gone to the party. Before learning to accept her husband's decisions, she would have pouted and made the evening miserable for both of them.

Encourage your husband to take the lead by being a good follower and telling him how much you enjoy his taking charge. As you display trust in his ability, he will generally become more eager to continue to be the head of the house. Interestingly, as you follow, your husband will be more prone to lead. But if you become aggressive, he may regress. If you nag, he may rebel. If you desire to please him, he will most likely want to please you. Efficiently fulfill your responsibilities to your husband, children, and home. Then your roles will be more clearly defined, and your husband may be more motivated to apply the same efficiency in his role. One lady commented, "As I have become a better wife, my husband has wanted to be a better husband. He can never be outdone."

Your husband can be head of the house, and you can still live under his protective leadership, even when he is absent, if you faithfully follow his wishes for you and the family. God's provision is marvelous. For instance, you may not always agree with him that your teenagers should be home early on weekend nights. Yet you can still make sure that they get in at the proper time when he is away on a business trip. You can tell them, "Dad wants you to be in by 11:00, so be sure to be home by then."

Ask God to show you any areas in which you have assumed your husband's roles. Then go to him and tell him you have been wrong in assuming the role God has given him. Be specific; name any areas in which you've taken over, such as disciplining the children, refusing to move when he was offered a promotion, or not following the budget. Tell him you know that since God gave him this role, God has equipped him to carry it out. Be sure to apologize for challenging his abilities by interfering. Assure him that you are aware of your failure. Tell him that you are excited and comforted by the knowledge that God will lead you through him. And amazing things will happen—in you, in him, and in your marriage as a whole.

Our daughter-in-love Melanie told our son Ken when he was offered a promotion out of state and far away from family and friends, that she simply would not move. As time went by, God spoke to her heart reminding her of His plan for the family order. After much inward wrestling, she apologized to her husband and said that she would support his decision realizing that God would give them His best. Ken was pleased! Their plans for moving were set into motion including putting their house on the market and house shopping. However, with the decline in the housing market, and the passing of time, Ken's heart was changed and new arrangements were made for his work. She accepted God's way and He gave her the desire of her heart including a deeper relationship with Ken. However, others have had to move. But in the move there are His wonderful compensations for those who walk with Him.

8

God's Best for You

Do you want God's best? This is an important question for you to settle. If you receive His best, you will experience peace of mind and heart:

"May the God of hope fill you with all joy and peace as you trust in Him, so that you may overflow with hope by the power of the Holy Spirit" (Romans 15:13).

God's joy, too, will be yours if you choose His best: *"But His joy is in those who reverence Him, those who expect Him to be loving and kind"* (Ps. 147:11 TLB).

Sarah, for example, chose God's best by responding to her husband, Abraham, as her authority. (See 1 Peter 3:5-6.) Through her submission, her beauty was accentuated.

God's best is also revealed through his Word. He offers us so much, as the psalmist reveals in Psalm 119:114: *"You are my refuge and my shield; I have put my hope in Your word."* As the Word reveals Jesus Christ and His will for you, it will be like a flashlight that lights your path ahead: *"Your word is a lamp to my feet and a light for my path"* (Ps. 119:105). The Bible is permanently established, and God will always honor and fulfill His Word. *"Your word, O Lord, is eternal; it stands firm in the heavens"* (Ps. 119:89). *"...For you have exalted above all things Your name and Your word"* (Ps. 138:2). The final authority in your life must be God's Word.

His protection of you is based on your performance of His will, not your will. God said through the prophet Isaiah, *"...If you want Me to protect you, you must learn to believe what I say"* (Isa. 7:9 TLB).

> The final authority in your life
> must be God's Word.

ABSOLUTE SUBMISSION

Because submission is such a core principle in God's design for our marriages, let's explore it in more depth.

In His kindness and grace, God makes it clear in His Word that He wants you to have a submissive attitude toward your husband. The apostle Paul wrote, *"Wives, submit to your husbands as to the Lord"* (Eph. 5:22). Many other verses emphasize the same thing (see 1 Pet. 3:1, 5-6; Gen. 3:16; 1 Cor. 11: 3, 8-9; 1 Tim. 2:11; Titus 2:2-5).

Translated, the word *submit* in Ephesians 5:22 suggests or implies continuous action. Submission is to be a way of life. We are never to stop submitting.

Although God has emphasized our need to submit, we still do it voluntarily. He does not force us to accept it any more than He forces us to receive His Son as our Savior. The phrase *"as to the Lord"* keeps this act of submission from being slavery and makes it a voluntary act of love. You might think of it this way. Our absolute submission is to the Lord and simply expressed to our husbands. Submission is an attitude. It is saying that I am teachable and want God's will more than my will. Submission is having our hearts and motives pure, yielded, surrendered, and abandoned to our God.

> The phrase **"as to the Lord"** keeps this act of submission from being slavery and makes it a voluntary act of love.

Submission is not just for women. *"Submit to one another out of reverence for Christ"* (Eph. 5:21) is the requirement God gave to both men and women. How to implement such submission is described in the following verses (Ephesians 5:22-23). The woman submits by respecting her husband, and the husband submits by loving his wife as he loves himself. As women, we can only fulfill our job description and leave our mates in God's hand. When this is our attitude, we can willingly submit to our husbands because we love the Lord and want to obey and please Him. When we willingly and lovingly submit to our husbands, our spirit of gentleness and love inspires our husbands to treat us gently and to cherish and protect us.

Notice, however, that none of the verses listed above read, "Be submissive if he is a Christian," or "if you can understand the outcome." No, God applies no such exceptions to our submission to our husbands.

 Submission is an attitude.

Have you ever heard of a woman disagreeing with the commandment, "You shall not steal"? (See Exodus 20:15.) I've never heard anyone say, "It is all right to steal if you are hungry, if no one sees you, or if you strongly desire an object." God undoubtedly did not intend for us to steal. We accept this commandment because He has made it clear. Yet women who would never consider

stealing frequently reject God's command to have a submissive spirit. If you are such a woman and are unwilling
to give God your total submission, do not allow the Lord
to be discredited by any blunders your attitude produces.
Admit you are living according to your plan, not His.

Most women I talk with want to be God's women and
to be in His will. You can be in the center of His will if you
have a submissive attitude toward the one whom God has
put in authority over you—your husband. You display
your submission to God when you display a teachable
attitude toward your husband's leadership. To refuse
to recognize your husband's leadership makes your life
incomplete and unsatisfying because you are breaking
God's command relating to this issue. Remember, you
do not degrade yourself or place yourself in an inferior
position when you recognize and respect your husband's
authority. Instead, you gain dignity, fulfillment, femininity, and freedom to be the woman God wants you to be.
God's plan is designed for your benefit!

Does complete submission to Jesus Christ through
your husband frighten you? Remember that *"the Lord is
fair in everything He does, and full of kindness"* (Ps. 145:17
TLB). Jesus Christ's love for you is so great and complete
that it is hard to understand. *"God demonstrates His own
love for us in this: While we were still sinners, Christ died for
us"* (Rom. 5:8). After dying for you, Jesus would not play
a dirty trick on you by putting you in a position that will
make you miserable. When I was first introduced to the
truth of being submissive to DeWitt as unto the Lord, I
thought, *No way will I do that!* My problem was that I did
not know who I was in Christ or what His heart for me was.
Over and over as I dared to allow God to work, I saw His
wisdom and love protecting me. The first time I can remember learning to trust God in this way happened when

our oldest son was only twelve. He had a paper route, was late coming home, and I feared he would get hit by a car riding home in the approaching darkness. When I told DeWitt that I was going in the car to get him, he said, "No, you let him ride home on his bicycle." My mother's heart silently protested. Then God reminded me of what I believed and taught. He said, "Can you trust me through your husband? Will you allow these truths to become reality now by trusting Me?" I said, "Yes, Lord." Within an hour our son came riding home. Through this I began learning that I could trust God for hard things not only for me, but also our son's confidence was strengthened by doing hard things on his own.

Do not put His love on the level of, or below, human love (which you do when you feel that He would repay submission with punishment).

> *Which of you, if his son asks for bread, will give him a stone? Or if he asks for a fish, will give him a snake? If you, then, though you are evil, know how to give good gifts to your children, how much more will your Father in heaven give good gifts to those who ask Him* (Matthew 7:9-11).

Suppose that when I return home after a trip, my sons greet me by saying, "Mother, we've missed you and have decided that we'll do anything you want us to do, starting now."

Imagine if I responded by saying, "Oh, good. I'm going to make your life miserable. You'll have brussel sprouts three times a day, and you'll never get to do anything you like to do again. You'll be sorry you made such a commitment to me."

Of course I wouldn't say that. Once I finished hugging my sons, I'd probably buy them presents. If we, in our incomplete human love, respond this way, surely we should not expect less from God. His love is perfect. He reaches out, wanting to minister to us in our deepest needs. If we can trust each other, surely we can trust the God of love and salvation.

> *We need have no fear of someone* [God] *who loves us perfectly; His perfect love for us eliminates all dread of what He might do to us. If we are afraid, it is for fear of what He might do to us, and shows that we are not fully convinced that He really loves us. So you see, our love for Him comes as a result of His loving us first* (1 John 4:18-19 TLB).

It should comfort each of us to know that God's will for us is to submit to our husbands. You see, God wants to use authority to expose our hearts so that we can make progress on the road to maturity. Our response to authority can be a vertical test to see if we want to hear from God, are willing to lay down our way in order to pursue His way, and are willing to let Him surprise us with His protection and blessings.

Watchman Nee, in his book *Spiritual Authority,* thoroughly explores this subject. He makes a statement with which I agree and believe sums up this issue: "Submission is absolute—obedience is relative."[1] We will discuss this idea further later in this chapter.

BE SUBMISSIVE IN EVERYTHING?

In Ephesians 5:24, God states, *"Now as the church submits to Christ, so also wives should submit to their husbands **in everything.**"* (Do not let the word *everything* shake you. The way that the Church submits to Christ in everything is the same way that we submit to our husbands.) You may immediately say, "You don't know my husband! He's not a Christian. He's unreasonable. That may work for some husbands and wives, but not for us." Do not, however, think you are an exception.

God deals with this specific problem:

Wives, in the same way be submissive to your husbands so that, if any of them do not believe the word, they may be won over without words by the behavior of their wives, when they see the purity and reverence of your lives (1 Peter 3:1-2).

Obviously the Lord is talking here to women whose husbands are not Christians.

> Your submission to your husband is part of God's plan for order in our world.

Your submission to your husband is part of God's plan for order in our world. (See 1 Peter 2:13-18.) The words *"in the same way"* in First Peter 3:1 refer back to First Peter 2:13-14,18:

Submit yourselves for the Lord's sake to every authority instituted among men: whether to the king as the supreme authority, or to governors, who are sent by him....Slaves, submit yourselves to your masters with all respect, not only to those who are good and considerate, but also to those who are harsh.

God is saying to you and me that His plan for us involves daily and joyful submission to our husbands, even as we would submit to governments or (in biblical times) a master. If we allow the Lord to cleanse us, fill us, and control us, and if we take a position of whole-hearted submission to our husbands because God has said we should, we can depend on God to fulfill His Word in caring for us and helping us to carry out His command.

Remember First Corinthians 10:13?

No temptation has seized you except what is common to man. God is faithful; He will not let you be tempted beyond what you can bear. But when you are tempted, He will also provide a way out so that you can stand up under it.

Now we don't know how God will fulfill His Word. We simply trust that He will. If our husbands have asked us to do something unreasonable, God may change their minds. As we noted earlier, *"The king's heart* [and your husband's] *is in the hand of the Lord; He directs it like a watercourse wherever He pleases"* (Prov. 21:1).

EXAMPLES OF LOVING SUBMISSION

Perhaps some true examples will help you understand God's gracious way of working things out for you when you obey Him and honor your husband.

Barbara had become a Christian, but her husband, Don, had not. She began to attend church faithfully and took the children. Don seemed bewildered at first by her new faith and interest in church. Then he became jealous and hurt because she was spending all their Sundays away from him. He did not feel as if he was number one in her life anymore.

Weeks later, Barbara heard these principles about submission to her husband, whether or not he was a Christian. Wanting to please the Lord, she decided to concentrate on honoring her husband. Easter Sunday morning came, and she and the children were all ready to go to church when Don woke up. Right away, she sensed that Don was unhappy. "Honey, would you like me to stay home with you today?" she asked. "You know I want to honor you. If you'd prefer to have me and the children home with you today, we'll stay here." He didn't answer, but she could tell that he wanted her to stay home. So she and the children changed into more casual clothes, and she planned some activities for them. As the morning progressed, her husband's mood got better and better. Later in the day, Don called the children to him. He picked up the Bible and said, "Children, I want us to read some of the Bible together." He read from Proverbs and talked to them about what God said.

Naturally Barbara's heart was warmed. She had given her husband his rightful place, and he was no longer jealous of her relationship with the church and Jesus Christ. Here he was, assuming spiritual leadership, and he wasn't a Christian! The day ended up being far better than an Easter service because the family was united in reading and discussing God's Word together in a God-orchestrated way. Later, there were other occasions when Barbara chose to stay home from church simply to give her husband his place in her life because God led her to do so. Could Barbara's decision to follow God's guidance in responding to her husband have been the key to his becoming a Christian a year later?

Allison had an experience much like Barbara's, only Allison had been raised to believe that to be spiritual she had to be in church for every activity. When the church doors were open, she went, quite self-righteously. But she had married Andy, who did not love Christ and did not care to attend church.

Allison's Sunday school teacher began to teach these biblical principles about the wife's role of submission. One Sunday she told Allison, "Your husband simply doesn't understand what's going on in your life. He's jealous. He cannot understand spiritual truths, and he wants you to stay home with him. Ask God to show you how to demonstrate to your husband that he has his rightful place in your heart."

Allison was shocked. She had never heard anything like that before. But when she saw that the principles of submission came right from God's Word, she agreed to try them. The next Sunday, she got herself and the children ready for church as usual. Andy, a traveling salesman, was sleeping late. He awoke, and after seeing her getting ready for church, began to rave, curse, and tell her he didn't see any difference in church people's lives or any good reason for her attending. So Allison quietly changed into casual dress.

"What are you doing?" Andy asked in amazement.

"Well, it's obvious you don't want me to go to church today," she said. "And I do love you. And I want to honor you. After all, I haven't spent much time with you since you've been going out of town. So it would be the right thing for me to stay home with you this morning. I'd like to hear what you've been doing this week, anyway."

Andy got out of bed and put his arms around her, tears filling his eyes. For the first time that morning, Allison saw something in Andy she had never seen before, just because she had put herself in the position God intended. God was able to bring out qualities in Andy she didn't know existed, and they had a happy day together.

As the weeks went by, Andy began attending church with her and the children. The last I heard, he still hadn't received Christ as Savior, but he still attended church with his family and encouraged them to do so—all because Allison's relationship with Christ and her church no longer threatened him.

Husbands don't normally want to be tyrannical or insensitive. They act that way because they feel insecure in their relationships with their wives and are fighting desperately to gain the position God meant them to have. Once a man sees that he doesn't have to fight for his wife's love and that he has her respect and full attention, he in turn will usually allow her to have her own activities and interests as long as she doesn't take advantage.

> Husbands don't normally want to be tyrannical or insensitive.

Perhaps your husband won't change in the ways Don and Andy did.

Laura's husband, Jake, gave her a bad time when she told him she was going to honor him and put him first in a way she hadn't before. He was not a Christian and decided to test her. "OK, Laura," he replied, "let's go to the Royal Three tonight." (It was an unsavory tavern.)

Laura was shaken, but didn't show Jake how she felt. "I said I'd defer to your requests, so I will," she told him.

He wouldn't believe her new attitude and kept creating new scenarios to test her. "Well, what will you do when such and such happens?"

"I'll take your requests seriously," she told him and proceeded to get ready. They were all dressed and ready to leave when he suddenly got a blinding headache. "Honey, I can't go," he told her. And they didn't. God had intervened.

Marilyn faced a similar situation. Her husband also asked her to go to a casino with him, and she went. However, she graciously refrained from taking part in questionable activities in such a way that she did not make her husband feel uncomfortable. Another woman, sitting nearby and watching, noticed that Marilyn wasn't taking part and came over to talk to her. Marilyn explained that she was refraining from the activities because of her faith in Jesus Christ, so she was able to glorify her Savior even at a casino. (Marilyn was strong enough to handle this assignment and not fall into questionable activities. Each person must evaluate such an assignment in that same light. Follow the direction that God gives you.)

Sally's problem wasn't as overwhelming. Her family was visiting her mother one day. Her mother offered Sally some rich dirt and plants to take home with her. Thankful, Sally got a big bucket and filled it full. But as she started to put it into the car, her husband, George, said, "You're not going to take that home in our clean car!"

"Why, George, I can put paper on the floor and hold the bucket so it won't spill," Sally answered.

"No, I don't want a dirty pail in the car," he told her. And that was that. Sally didn't argue because she knew these principles of showing respect to her husband.

Figuring she'd return later in the truck and get the dirt, she just forgot about the incident. But as they were getting ready to leave, her husband surprised her. "Oh, go ahead and get the bucket of dirt," he said. "If you hold it like you promised, it should be OK."

This little incident made Sally think back to other times in their relationship. She realized that George felt at times as if he were no longer the head of the house. She could see that when he felt sure of himself and not threatened, he was kind and compassionate. He had simply needed to be taken seriously and to have his leadership honored.

So many marital problems result from a misunderstanding of the husband-wife relationship or from the wife's deliberate refusal to honor and respect her husband. It is significant that six verses in First Peter 3:1-7 speak to the wife about her role, and only one verse instructs the husband. The woman's role is crucial, strategic, and often hard to fill. God takes extra time instructing the woman on how to fulfill that role so she won't go to an extreme and become like a slave, but will still retain her individuality and her husband's love.

> The woman's role is crucial, strategic, and often hard to fill.

Let's not forget that God's Word coupled with the leadership of the Holy Spirit is our protection. There God has outlined the fact that He wants us to submit by honoring and respecting our husbands as a way of life. If we do, we can depend on God to keep His Word and to deal with our husbands in whatever way He sees necessary.

YOUR ATTITUDES AND MOTIVES MATTER

God holds you responsible for your attitude and motives concerning Him and your husband. You must be transparent before God. He cannot be fooled. *"...The Lord does not look at the things man looks at. Man looks at the outward appearance, but the Lord looks at the heart"* (1 Sam. 16:7). Do not attempt to rationalize or justify your actions. *"We can justify our every deed, but God looks at our motives"* (Prov. 21:2 TLB). It is relaxing and comforting to be open and honest with God. He loves you! He wants the best for you, your husband, and your marriage.

Make every effort not to play games with your husband, either. He can sense if you submit willingly or grudgingly. Do not be like the little boy whose father told him to sit down in his seat at the table. The little boy refused. Finally, the father threatened to take away his dinner if he would not obey. The boy sat down, but mumbled under his breath, "I'll sit down, but I'm still standing up on the inside." You cannot afford to "stand up on the inside." Such rebellion will destroy your joy and your husband's.

Remember, your husband's unreasonable demands or actions, whether or not he is a Christian, can be stimulated or minimized by your attitudes. That is why it is so important for you to voluntarily submit to him with pure motives.

God's Word reminds us that husbands may be won to the Lord *"when they see the purity and reverence of our lives"* (1 Peter 3:2). So, your husband will notice that you don't fall apart over things that used to upset you. He will observe that when he stays out longer with the guys, you don't go into a tailspin, have a tantrum, or nag him for days. You give him his freedom and accept him the way he is. He will see that you do not *"give way to fear"* (1 Pet. 3:6) and that you have more patience with the children. You'll get his attention when you're more thoughtful and considerate of him, when you listen to him and think about him, when you respect and reverence him, when you adore and admire him, when you praise him and sincerely enjoy his company.

When your husband sees and lives with this kind of woman, he cannot help but be influenced! He cannot help but be softened and stimulated to become the man God means him to be. So, it is your responsibility as a wife to fulfill the role God designed for you, keeping your relationship with your husband right and leaving everything else to God. Trust Him to deal with your husband and work out difficulties in the ways he sees best. God longs for you to trust Him.

Your attitude is an important key to your success with your husband. If you do not want to submit to your husband, I encourage you to confess this to the Lord. Trust Him to control your life and change your desires. You will be thrilled to see God's Word become a living reality in your mind.

What About My Reputation?

The wise wife will focus her mind on obeying God as we have discussed. Her primary consideration will be to build a successful marriage, not to look around and see what others think about what she's doing or to regulate her life in order to please others. In other words, if in obeying your husband and putting him first, you must go to a casino with him, do not worry about what others will say. Nor should you worry if you can't attend church every Sunday. In other words, do not be concerned about gossip or listen to well-meaning, but wrong, marital advice, even when it comes from Christian friends.

Your responsibility is to do the will of God, not to seek approval from others. Jesus said,

> *"By Myself I can do nothing; I judge only as I hear, and My judgment is just, for I seek not to please Myself but Him* [the Father] *who sent me"* (John 5:30).

If Jesus could say that He had come to do God's will, not His own, certainly you and I should put God's will first in our lives, too.

Jesus' reputation was not good in some religious circles. Some religious people accused Him of being a drunk (see Luke 7:34). Others said, in effect, "What kind of man is this who keeps company with tax collectors, prostitutes, and sinners?" (See Matthew 11:19.) Jesus *"made Himself nothing, taking the very nature of a servant, being made in human likeness"* (Phil. 2:7).

Mary, the mother of Jesus, had a bad reputation among those who did not believe in the virgin birth. It has been said that one reason Joseph took Mary with him to Bethlehem during the year of Jesus' birth was to protect her from gossip at home. Even today, some call Jesus the illegitimate son of Mary.

Some Christians may be upset if you do not attend all church functions. They may quote Hebrews 10:25 to you, where it says Christians should not neglect assembling together. If they are critical, simply tell them you are only refraining for a time so you can return to church later with your husband's blessing—and hopefully with him. Think of this as a sacrifice that you lay at Jesus' feet at His leading.

Of course, you should study your Bible faithfully so God can speak to you and guide you when you cannot attend church. You might even ask a friend for a recording of the worship services so you can enjoy them during your personal time with the Lord. You may attend a daytime women's Bible study or find other opportunities to assemble for Christian fellowship.

If we are Christians, we belong to Jesus Christ. We can trust Him to care for us. The psalmist David wrote, *"He restores my soul; He guides me in paths of righteousness for His name's sake"* (Ps. 23:3). It is His reputation that is at stake when you obey Him and your husband, not yours.

SHADOWS IN THE DARK

Although your imagination and worries can create many questions and fears, do not become upset about someone else's situation or some unknown possibility. Worrying about "what ifs" is not trusting God. Jesus promises to be sufficient for all those who trust in Him for their present problems. *"God...is faithful"* (1 Cor. 1:9); *"Cast all your anxiety on Him because He cares for you"* (1 Pet. 5:7). Let the light of Jesus Christ dissolve all your fears or "shadows in the dark"!

GUIDELINES IN ACCOMPLISHING GOD'S WILL

Sometimes the concept of "doing God's will" can seem overwhelming. Here are some guidelines to help you:

Recognize the Value of Problems

Your role of submission to your husband will become an exciting adventure when you realize that one of the reasons for this role is to develop a mature spiritual attitude. God desires for His children to become like Jesus Christ.

> *"For from the very beginning God decided that those who came to Him—and all along He knew who would— should become like His Son, so that His Son would be the First, with many brothers"* (Romans 8:29 TLB).

God wants to use any situation in which you find yourself to make you like Jesus so you *"are being transformed into His likeness with ever-increasing glory"* (2 Cor. 3:18).

Is there any area in which you are having problems with your husband? Has it occurred to you that God may want to use this to overcome a weakness in you? Because of our carnal flesh, every person has a strong will. When the sin nature is in control of your life, your marriage will suffer. So what can you do? Romans 6:11-12 says, *"Count yourselves dead to sin but alive to God in Christ Jesus. Therefore do not let sin reign in your mortal body...."* When we exchange our desires for Christ's, the initial pain of dying to self is a healing pain that is followed by peace and fulfillment. When we are unwilling to exchange our desires for Christ's, we experience a kind of pain that produces unhealed heartaches.

Jesus never promised problem-free lives. *"The good man does not escape all troubles—he has them too. But the Lord helps him in each and every one"* (Ps. 34:19 TLB). James wrote:

> *Consider it pure joy...whenever you face trials of many kinds, because you know that the testing of your faith develops perseverance....Blessed is the man who perseveres under trial, because when he has stood the test,*

he will receive the crown of life that God has promised to those who love Him (James 1:2-3, 12).

Problems are for our benefit when we turn to God.

Consider Your Husband's Position

Your husband is a tool in the Father's hand. You are to honor and respect his position, not necessarily all aspects of his personality. Your husband may not understand you and may have personality deficiencies that bother you, but God promises that He is able to work through these deficiencies more effectively as your attitude pleases Him. *"When a man's ways are pleasing to the Lord, He makes even his enemies live at peace with him"* (Prov. 16:7). If God can enable you to live with an enemy peacefully, He certainly can help you live at peace with an ornery husband. When a problem comes up, ask yourself, *What is God saying to me through this situation?* You and I could miss many valuable lessons by not responding in this way to our difficulties. God sees weak areas in our lives—areas we are often unaware of—and wants to help us. The psalmist wrote, *"...For all my ways are known to You"* (Ps. 119:168).

> If God can enable you to live with an enemy peacefully, He certainly can help you live at peace with an ornery husband.

For example, Jesus had to take me through a particular lesson many times before I saw what He wanted to teach me. DeWitt had often expressed disapproval when I talked on the phone frequently while he was home. I thought he was being unfair. Finally the Lord got through to me and showed me that my behavior expressed more concern for the feelings of others than for my husband. Realizing what my actions implied, I saw how wrong I was. My stubbornness in not seeing earlier what God wanted to teach me had caused much unnecessary friction.

Find Out Your Husband's Real Motives

Finding out what your husband's real motives are will help you be a helpmate who shows respect to him. For instance, why doesn't he want you to buy the dress you are so crazy about? Does he want to hurt you, or is he considering the family budget?

If your husband drinks excessively or has another habit or addiction that affects his reason, find out what his basic goals are or his wishes in specific instances and obey these, not his unreasonable demands when he is drunk or obsessed. If you don't support him when he is "under the influence," you are not disobeying him in this instance, but are carrying out instructions he gave you when he was thinking clearly. Let me share an illustration.

Chris seemed to have no control over his desire to gamble. At times he won tremendous sums of money; other times, he lost everything he had. Finally he realized that his gambling could hurt his wife, children, and himself. One day, right after winning a large sum of money, he went to his lawyer and had him put the winnings in savings. "I want you to draw up some kind of contract that says I can never touch this money," Chris said. "It's for my children's future and any immediate needs my wife might have." If I come to you on my knees, begging you to break the contract and get the money, don't listen to me." He then said something similar to his wife. Later, he did beg his wife to get some of the money out of savings, but she refused, knowing that in his "right frame of mind" he did not want her to touch that money except in real need.

God the Holy Spirit will enable you to creatively respond to situations. You'll be surprised at the alternatives He will give you in following your husband's directions while maintaining personal convictions.

Coming home tired from work, your husband may say, "Tell anyone who calls that I'm not home." What is his motive for asking you to say this? Obviously he does not want to be disturbed; it isn't that he is forcing you to lie. Therefore, you can tell him that you'll be glad to handle the calls so that he won't be disturbed. You can respond to those who call with, "May I have your name and number? My husband will call when it's convenient."

Choose your words carefully when responding creatively to your husband's requests. You must not project disapproval of him or make him feel guilty. Obedience to God's Word will help develop your common sense and good judgment. *"Now teach me good judgment as well as knowledge,"* the psalmist wrote. *"For Your laws are my guide"* (Ps. 119:66 TLB).

Be Patient and Trust God to Change Your Husband's Mind

When your husband makes a wrong decision, remember that God is bigger than your husband or your circumstances, so give God time to change your husband's mind. Remember, God *"changes times and seasons;*

he sets up kings and deposes them. He gives wisdom to the wise and knowledge to the discerning" (Dan. 2:21).

Do not be surprised at what God may use to change your husband's mind! After DeWitt decided to purchase a motorcycle, several months elapsed before God changed his mind about it. God used this period of time to teach me about His faithfulness. Without too much difficulty, I had been able to trust Christ concerning DeWitt's buying a motorcycle for himself, but when he talked about buying a minibike for our young sons, I felt he was going too far! I exercised my privilege of sharing my feelings about the many dangers of motorcycling. He seemed to agree, and I thought the matter was settled. Later, however, he exercised his right to overrule my decision and bought the boys a minibike anyway. I knew I needed to accept his decision and trust God for the results. I placed the boys' safety in God's hands and, by faith, entered into their joy.

Weeks later, DeWitt had a freak accident as he rode into our driveway one evening. He hurt his knee just enough to convince him of the dangers of motorcycling. He sold the motorcycle three days later and then decided not to repair a hole that appeared soon afterward in the minibike's engine. When God changes a person's mind, He does it completely.

Expect pressure while God is working to change your husband's mind. Your husband may give you a bad time just to see if you really intend to support a decision of his with which you disagree. Trust Christ's sufficiency during such pressures. *"Praise be to the Lord my Rock....He is my loving God and my fortress, my stronghold and my deliverer, my shield, in whom I take refuge"* (Ps. 144:1-2). God will use these pressures to develop strong character in you. The apostle Paul, who was no stranger to hardship, wrote, *"We also rejoice in our sufferings, because we know that suffering produces perseverance; perseverance, character; and character, hope"* (Rom. 5:3-4).

Each member of your family can develop strong character through problems and trials just as you can. It's so easy to do more harm than good by overly protecting your loved ones. They can learn valuable lessons through mistakes, suffering, or trouble that they cannot learn any other way. Don't rob them of such opportunities.

OBEDIENCE IS RELATIVE

The truth of submission is one of the most important truths in our Christian walk. It is also one of the most misunderstood truths and one of the most difficult to communicate. Submission and obedience seem to get wrongly interwined.

When I read the statement "submission is absolute—obedience is realtive" in Watchman Nee's book *Spriitual Authority,* I knew he had made clear a misunderstood truth. Submission is absolute because it describes our relationship to God, which is to be one of total abandonment. Others benefit as we live such a life with our God.

What does "obedience is realtive" mean then? It means that I may or may not obey a given request depending on two factors. First, does the request violate God's Word? Second, does it violate my God-inspired conscience?

The biblical incident of Daniels' friends disobeying King Nebuchadnezzar is an excellent illustration of these truths. Shadrach, Meshach, and Abednego submissively refused to obey the king's ungodly command to worship a golden idol. They submitted to authority even though it meant being thrown into the fiery furnace. God met them in a special way. The fire touched nothing except the ropes that bound them. (Read the details of the exciting adventure in Daniel 3.) Others, such as the ones who "overcame" (see Heb 11:36-40), have not been spared the consequences of their godly decisions.

Just as we are not to obey an ungodly request, it is also godly to take a stand against abuse. Our heavenly Father never desired that anyone be abused. Abuse happens because individuals who do not submit to Jesus' lordship misuse the free will God gave them. Free will was given to us not so that we can do as we please, but rather so we can explore the depths of God's love. If we condone abuse or don't stand against it, we can be partially guilty by being an accomplice to the abuser's activity or behavior.

Do we intercede for the abuser and resist the enemy by not enabling the behavior and praying the person will see the light and repent? Yes. How long and how much will be according to the leading of the Lord in each individual situation. No one can decide for another when enough is enough. His grace for the one in an unpleasant situation may not be understood by the one outside. Each person must be led by God's Spirit.

GODLY STAND

Here are a few guidelines to consider when taking a godly stand:

You did not cause your husband to be abusive. His behavior came out of his own unregenerate heart (see

Mark 7:15,21). It may be true that your expectations and your behavior may need some radical changing. But your husband must take full responsibility for his own sinful actions and reactions. He is accountable for his choices. You are called to deal with your sin only.

You cannot save your husband. Pray that the eyes of his heart will be enlightened (see Eph. 3:18) and that he will be strengthened in his spirit (see Eph. 3:16). Continue to love him as best you can. But don't fall for the thinking that if you just love him enough he will be all right. He needs Jesus' love, and he may need a counselor or a godly friend who can objectively help him get to the root of his behavior.

Submission does not mean that you should condone or receive abuse. You are a child of God, and you honor Him by esteeming yourself enough to say to an abusive husband, "Your behavior is not acceptable. I love you too much to let you continue in this pattern. I will not enable you to sow more and more fleshly seeds that you will eventually reap." (See Galatians 6:7-8.) You may simply walk out of the room or require him to get counseling. Sometimes a separation (if the situation is critical) for the purpose of reconciliation is an incentive for a reluctant or abusive husband to pursue help (see 1 Cor. 7:11). Such a stand must be the result of much prayer and must be led by the Spirit of God. Be careful to maintain your umbrella of protection by staying under your pastor's authority during such critical times. During such emotional times we need objective, godly perspective.

Just as we can submissively disobey an ugodly request, we can respectfully confront fleshly behavior. Such actions should be with a spirit of gentleness, as Galatians 6:1 describes.[2]

DELIGHT IN THE LORD

When you *"delight yourself in the Lord...He will give you the desires of your heart. Commit your way to the Lord; trust in Him..."* (Ps. 37:4-5). The key is to delight yourself in the Lord, not in your desires. You must operate according to God's plan and timetable, not yours.

Be prepared! God may change your desires. When DeWitt and I bought new bedroom furniture, I wanted a nightstand, but DeWitt said we did not need one. My immediate response was one of rebellion. Then I committed my desire to the Lord, and God changed my desire to correspond with DeWitt's. One cannot lose when pursuing God's plan.

As you apply these insights and are submissive to your husband *"as to the Lord,"* you will be able to share David's response to the Lord: *"Great is our Lord and mighty in power; His understanding has no limit"* (Ps. 147:5).

ENDNOTES

1. Nee, Watchman. *Spiritual Authority.* New York, NY: Christian Fellowship Publishers, Inc., 1972, 107.

2. Information found in Paula Sandford, *Healing Women's Emotions.* Tulsa, OK: Victory House, 1992, 45-47, greatly influenced and contributed to this section on abuse. Other resources on abuse and healthy living include Melody Beattie. Codependent No More. Hazelden Foundation, 1987 and Elijah House Ministries, www.elijahhouse.org. www.harvesthome.org. www.RestoringTheFoundations.org. www.shiloplace.org.

9

Timeless Beauty

It's no secret that men have different views of beauty. One man will marry a quiet, shy woman. Another will marry a bold, outgoing woman. Yet another will marry a glamorous type. But no matter what we looked like when we got married, we all know that as we age, our physical beauty will change. We'll get wrinkles. We'll sag in new places. Our skin will change, as will our hips.

Most women would give almost anything to have a beauty that improves instead of fades as they mature. Yet every woman who belongs to Christ inherits that kind of beauty! God describes this beauty in First Peter 3:4: *"It should be that of your inner self, the unfading beauty of a gentle and quiet spirit, which is of great worth in God's sight."* Incorruptible or timeless beauty begins on the inside, and its radiance actually transforms your outward appearance.

Fadeless beauty is what a mature man looks for in a wife. The sparkle in your eyes, a warm smile, a radiant and fresh, feminine manner, and a gentle and peaceful spirit mean more to your man than your external features, although it is still important to care for your physical body. But your inner beauty will be evident only when you realize that you are worthwhile and valuable in God's eyes. You are not "second-rate." Don't get hung up on unchangeable features you consider ugly, such as a large nose or ears, a long face, or extreme height. When tempted to worry about such characteristics, remember that you had them when your husband chose you. They are part of the whole you he loves. Thank God for them, knowing that they have a purpose in God's plan for your life. As you trust Him, He will use your features for your benefit. After all, if you are a Christian, you are royalty—a daughter of the King! You are in God's family (see 1 John 3:1). Jesus shed His blood for you (see 1 Pet. 1:18-19; Rom. 5:8), and He loves you very much (see Rom. 8:37-39). Being aware of your true value because of what Christ has done for you will enable you to gain self-respect and self-esteem.

> Fadeless beauty is what a
> mature man looks for in a wife.

The source of your incorruptible beauty, that which comes from within, is the spiritual condition of your heart: *"For as he thinks in his heart, so is he"* (Prov. 23:7 NKJV). Proverbs 4:23 states, *"Above all else, guard your heart, for it is the wellspring of life."* Jesus said, *"...For out of the overflow of the heart the mouth speaks"* (Matt. 12:34). We are challenged to love the Lord with all our hearts (see Matt. 22:37). And Peter challenged a sorcerer by saying, *"Your heart is not right before God"* (Acts 8:9-21).

When your heart is right before God, filled with His truth and love, your eyes and features will express a gentle nature and peaceful outlook. Lovely attitudes dominating your heart will show up as pleasant expressions on your face. Sparkling eyes, a warm smile, and relaxed facial muscles are symptoms of a good "heart" condition. In contrast, dull or angry eyes, harsh lines of the lips, and a scowl are symptoms of a bad "heart" condition. Only Jesus Christ, the Master Physician, can improve the condition of your heart. Without Him, your heart will remain under sin's control, full of sin and a fountain of evil (see Jer. 17:9; Matt. 12:35; 15:18-19). Your natural thoughts are influenced by the world's system, and your sin nature is opposed to God.

In Ephesians 4:17-18, our natural, sinful state is called darkness: "

> *...You must no longer live as the Gentiles do, in the futility of their thinking. They are darkened in their understanding and separated from the life of God because of the ignorance that is in them....* "

The only solution to this spiritual darkness (wrong thoughts, attitudes, and actions) is the transforming light of Jesus Christ that produces true beauty. Jesus said, *"I am the light of the world. Whoever follows Me will never walk in darkness, but will have the light of life"* (John 8:12).

You may think, *Jesus Christ is no longer present on earth in bodily form to be my light.* You are right. He is now seated *"at the right hand of the throne of God"* (Heb. 12:2). Yet, though presently at the right hand of the Father, Jesus has left total provision for you through His Word and the indwelling Holy Spirit (see John 16:7). He is the Living Word: *"In the beginning was the Word* [Christ], *and the Word was with God, and the Word was God"* (John 1:1). Remember that He wants to relive His life in and through us by the power of the Holy Spirit. In this way, His words are fulfilled, *"...the works that I do he will do also; and greater works than these he will do, because I go to My Father"* (John 14:12).

Christ has left the written Word, His inspired thoughts in writing, to give us direction and to show us His will. He, the Living Word, makes His written Word alive to us so that we know how to apply it to our individual situations. His Word is like a personal letter to us. He promises those of us who are Christians that *"...we have the mind of Christ"* (1 Cor. 2:16). As we look to Jesus, He will give us wisdom and revelation so we can know Him better (see Eph. 1:17).

Our heavenly Father wants each of us—as daughters of the King—to have inner beauty that comes from knowing Him better. As the psalmist wrote, *"The King* [God] *is enthralled by your beauty; honor Him, for He is your lord"* (Ps. 45:11).

GOD'S BEAUTY SALON

Your inner beauty will develop as you maintain a daily appointment with God in His "beauty salon." His beauty treatment is available without cost to all who want fadeless beauty and come to Him for treatment. Treatment involves acknowledging your need for Him, studying the Bible regularly, and obeying the biblical principles He reveals through studying, talking with Him in prayer, enjoying companionship with Him, and participating with what He is doing.

God works to develop your beauty as you surrender to Him much as you would surrender to the hands of a local beauty operator. *"Let the beauty and delightfulness and favor of the Lord our God be upon us..."* (Ps. 90:17 AMP). His beauty treatment involves sitting under His beauty lamp and letting it clear up the defects in your life—transforming the darkness in your soul to the light of beauty. As you submit to God and begin your beauty

142

treatment, realize that your natural thoughts and ways of doing things are opposed to His thoughts and ways.

"For My thoughts are not your thoughts, neither are your ways My ways," saith the Lord. "For as the heavens are higher than the earth, so are My ways higher than your ways, and My thoughts than your thoughts" (Isaiah 55:8-9 KJV).

THE POWER OF GOD'S WORD

As you read God's Word, you must decide whether or not you will believe it. If your response is positive, God the Holy Spirit, who lives in a believer, will use this knowledge to illuminate your soul or inner self. The light of God's Word will chase away the gloom of sin, cleansing you and making you like Jesus Christ. How powerful is God's Word?

The word of God is living and active. Sharper than any double-edged sword, it penetrates even to dividing soul and spirit, joints and marrow; it judges the thoughts and attitudes of the heart (Hebrews 4:12).

Let the word of Christ dwell in you richly... (Colossians 3:16).

For everything that was written in the past was written to teach us, so that through endurance and the encouragement of the Scriptures we might have hope (Romans 15:4).

God's Word (wisdom), as described in Proverbs 4:9, *"will set a garland of grace on your head and present you with a crown of splendor."*

As you read God's Word, you must decide whether or not you will believe it.

If you say no to God's Word, its principles may re-remain in your mind as intellectual knowledge, but will not transform you. But if through reading and meditating on God's Word you allow Christ's mind to be formed in your own and you operate on the basis of God's principles, you will experience stability, inner peace, fulfillment, and inner beauty.

You can know whether you are saying yes or no to God's Word by your application (or lack of application) of God's Word to your daily situations. For instance, God said in First Peter 5:7 that you are not to worry, but are to let Him take care of your problems. If you refuse to give Him your problems, saying, "Anyone would be upset in my situation," or "It's my nature to worry," you are living according to human principles for life, not God's.

God's powerful Word can reduce or eliminate your anxiety as you realize that God has provided for every circumstance in your life. He knows everything about everyone. Everything about us is wide open to His all-seeing eyes. *"Great is our Lord and mighty in power; His understanding has no limit"* (Ps. 147:5). God Himself said, through the prophet, *"I the Lord search the heart and examine the mind..."* (Jer. 17:10).

God not only knows all things, but He has already provided victory for you over every situation you will ever face (see 1 Cor. 10:13; 15:57). And the light of His Word is sufficient for all of life's paths: *"Your Word is a lamp to my feet and a light for my path"* (Ps. 119:105).

God's Word is also like a mirror, revealing sinful defects in your beauty (see James 1:23-26). Those defects grieve the Holy Spirit (see Eph. 4:30) and dim your transforming light of beauty. Your confession of sins returns the Holy Spirit to full control of your life so that the light (God's Word) can shine into all areas of your life and transform you into the image of Jesus Christ (see 1 John 1:9).

> *Therefore, I urge you, brothers, in view of God's mercy, to offer your bodies as living sacrifices, holy and pleasing to God—this is your spiritual act of worship. Do not conform any longer to the pattern of this world, but be transformed by the renewing of your mind. Then you will be able to test and approve what God's will is...* (Romans 12:1-2).

THE POWER OF PRAYER

Prayer is also an important part of God's beauty treatment. Jesus said, *"If you remain in Me and My words remain in you, ask whatever you wish, and it will be given to you"* (John 15:7). The Message by Eugene H. Peterson states this truth as, *"Whatever you request along the lines of who I am and what I am doing, I'll do it."* Jesus also said, *"...Ask, and you will receive, and your joy will be complete"* (John 16:24). He also said, *"Pray continually"* (1 Thess. 5:17). To pray continually, among other things, can refer to an attitude of prayer as a way of life. As you walk in His presence, enjoying companionship with Him, when He directs your attention to a matter, you simply agree with Him, thereby participating in what He's doing. Pray about everything (see Phil. 4:6-7), and you will know His peace—another wonderful beauty aid.

As you share your praise, your requests, and your needs with God through prayer in Jesus' name, God promises to hear, answer, and fill you with joy. And joy can transform the plainest face into a radiant one!

True, you must meet some conditions for an effective prayer life. King David gave us an example.

"Search me [thoroughly], O God, and know my heart! Try me, and know my thoughts! And see if there is any wicked or hurtful way in me, and lead me in the way everlasting" (Psalm 139:23-24 AMP).

Should He reveal any defects, agree with Him and release that area to Him for cleansing, healing, and transformation.

Certainly if you spend time in God's beauty salon, reading His Word and letting it do its work in your life, and if you take time to pray, God's radiance will shine in your face and personality. No beauty can compare to beauty like this!

Nurture Emotional Stability in Yourself

Developing emotional stability will also add to your timeless beauty. One way to maintain emotional balance is to develop a sense of humor. Do not take yourself too seriously. *"A cheerful heart is good medicine..."* (Prov. 17:22). *"...The cheerful heart has a continual feast [regardless of circumstances]"* (Prov. 15:15). You are to your family's atmosphere what a thermostat is to the temperature of your home. If you are relaxed about life, your home will have a relaxed atmosphere. If you can laugh with your husband and laugh at yourself, for example, your home will be a happier place. DeWitt has often said, "If Momma ain't happy, no one is happy!" Even though he is being humorous, there is an element of truth in this saying. My emotions have often controlled me, bleeding over into all my affairs. What a joy to learn that Jesus wants to release His self-control through me. I have enjoyed learning to let Him use my emotions to expose privately an area of healing that is needed. Then with my family expresses His joy, I laugh at myself and trust Him to heal me. It works! Our attitude is contagious.

> One way to maintain
> emotional balance
> is to develop a sense of humor.

Certainly there will be times when routine household tasks, mistakes in household management, routine childcare problems, decisions regarding meals, or other things cause you to become discouraged. Be honest with your husband as is appropriate, but also remember to ask God for strength and guidance. The apostle Paul wrote,

> *Work hard and cheerfully at all you do, just as though you were working for the Lord and not merely for your masters, remembering that it is the Lord Christ who is going to pay you, giving you your full portion of all He owns. He is the one you are really working for* (Colossians 3:23-24 TLB).

These words, addressed to servants, apply to anyone who has tasks to perform.

Another key component of emotional stability is a grateful attitude, which you will develop through Christ's power in your life as you live in His presence. *"Let the peace of Christ rule in your hearts....And be thankful"* (Col. 3:15). You can be thankful for every person in your life as you realize that Christ promises to work out all things (or use any person) for your benefit as you trust Him. If you have a thankful spirit, your husband will enjoy your company more and be more likely to become the husband you need and want.

Let gratitude be your response, for example, when your husband gives you a gift. Remember that he and his thoughtfulness are more important than what he gives you. Therefore accept his gifts with a joyful spirit and sincere appreciation. If you are always returning his gifts, that can discourage him from gift giving.

What if he does not give you gifts? Examine your past actions to see if you have violated any of the principles we have mentioned. If not, you simply may be married to a man who does not enjoy shopping. (By the way, few men do.) Accept him as he is! And don't allow yourself to become upset about this.

You also foster emotional stability when you understand how to ask your husband for what you want or need. Do not hint. (Men are usually so preoccupied with their activities that they do not catch subtle hints. Then their wives feel hurt, thinking their men do not love them.) Avoid trying to convince him of your need in order to get your way. He may feel trapped and rebel. Demanding your way does not work either because in demanding you are usurping his authority, and he may feel offended by your actions. Instead, ask for things with a simple "May I, please?" or "Will you, please?" When you use this simple straightforward method, don't be surprised if you find him more willing to grant your requests. Of course, be careful not to ask for things he and the family as a whole cannot afford.

Deadly Traps That Mar Your Beauty

The beauty that God is creating in you and revealing through you can be marred when anger, fear, or depression control your life. Sinful emotions cannot control you without damaging your beauty and your physical and spiritual health. Medical studies have shown that these emotions are key factors in producing many illnesses. Dr. Caroline Leaf states, "Research shows that around 87% of illnesses can be attributed to our thought life, and approximately 13% to diet, genetics and environment. Studies conclusively link more chronic diseases (also known as lifestyle disease) to an epidemic of toxic emotions in our culture."[1] Since you do not want your beauty to be marred, let's explore what God's Word reveals about these deadly emotions and the traps they can create.

Anger

Anger takes many forms, including envy, intolerance, criticism, revenge, hatred, rebellion, jealousy, and unforgiveness. Some of these forms of anger are mentioned in Ephesians 4:31: *"Get rid of all bitterness, rage, and anger, brawling and slander, along with every form of malice."* God commands you not to be controlled by these sinful emotions that flow from your sin nature because He wants you to be joyful and beautiful. Look at yourself in the mirror when you are angry and see how your beauty is blemished.

A wife controlled by Jesus Christ is a crowning joy to her husband, but when she is controlled by anger, her presence can be torture: *"Better to live on a corner of the roof than share a house with a quarrelsome wife....Better to live in a desert than with a quarrelsome and ill-tempered wife"* (Prov. 21:9,19).

One form of torture is the continual dropping of water on one's head. The Bible suggests that an angry wife is like this hellish torment. *"A quarrelsome wife is like constant dripping on a rainy day"* (Prov. 27:15; see also Prov. 19:13; 25:24). God needs to give a command only once to emphasize its importance. The fact that He refers various times to the repugnance of an angry wife should warn us of the seriousness of anger. God does not want us to miss the point.

Anger has a way of multiplying and reproducing itself in the lives of our husbands and children. Could outbursts of anger from our family members be caused or influenced by our own (perhaps unconscious) bad attitudes or moods?

The usual cause of anger is identified by the ugly word *selfishness.* When we become angry, it is usually because we feel that our rights have been violated. Or we want something done for us that has not been done, or we do not want something done that has been done. We can excuse and justify our weaknesses and even indulge in vengeful, bitter feelings, but the underlying cause is still selfishness. Whatever our justifications may be for our anger, it's important for us to apologize to those we've wronged, confess our sins to God, and trust Him to change us.

> Anger has a way of multiplying
> and reproducing itself in
> the lives of our husbands and children.

Should our anger be directed toward one who has wrongfully violated us, such anger can be understood. However, we must take the necessary steps to lay the offense and the person at Jesus' feet and let Him avenge us rather than taking it into our own hands by holding on to the anger (see Rom. 12:19).

FEAR

Fear is an emotional trap that is as damaging to your beauty and overall health as anger. No kind of makeup will cover the self-consciousness, doubts, and fears reflected on your face. Fear may be displayed through anxiety, doubt, timidity, indecision, superstition, withdrawal, loneliness, aggression, worry, feelings of inferiority, cowardice, hesitance, depression, haughtiness, and shyness.

> No kind of makeup will cover the self-consciousness, doubts, and fears reflected on your face.

What causes fear? It may be caused by a conscience that is guilty because of sin. Adam and Eve's first eating of the forbidden fruit brought fear.

Then the man and his wife heard the sound of the Lord God as He was walking in the garden in the cool of the day, and they hid from the Lord God among the trees of the garden. But the Lord God called to the man, "Where are you?" He [Adam] answered, "I heard You in the garden, and I was afraid because I was naked; so I hid" (Genesis 3:8-10).

Sin caused them to hide, fearing and running from the presence of the Lord, whereas before their sin they enjoyed God's presence and fellowship.

Sin produces fear from which we try to escape, physically or mentally. *"The wicked man flees though no one pursues, but the righteous are as bold as a lion"* (Prov. 28:1). We do not have to prove or justify ourselves if we are not guilty. We need not be afraid if we are innocent.

> *There is no fear in love. But perfect love drives out fear, because fear has to do with punishment. The one who fears is not made perfect in love* (1 John 4:18).

> *Dear friends, if our hearts do not condemn us, we have confidence before God* (1 John 3:21).

If you have fearful feelings of guilt, ask God or seek counsel from a godly person to determine if you have actually violated God's Word or if these feelings stem from past abuse or painful, unhealed experiences. Compare your actions and thoughts with God's Word in order to determine your true spiritual condition. If God's Word reveals your guilt, confess your sin, thank Jesus for paying the penalty for it when He died for you on the cross, and receive His forgiveness. The Father forgives your sin because of Christ's work for you. *"As far as the east is from the west, so far has he removed our transgressions from us"* (Ps. 103:12). Do not look back or remember the sin again. Let it be a closed case. God has forgiven you.

Fear may also come from not knowing or not believing God's Word. Peter's lack of faith in Christ, for example, caused him terror:

> *In the fourth watch* [between three and six o'clock] *of the night Jesus went out to them, walking on the*

lake. When the disciples saw Him walking on the lake, they were terrified. "It's a ghost!" they said, and cried out in fear. But Jesus immediately said to them: "Take courage! It is I. Don't be afraid!" "Lord, if it's You," Peter replied, "tell me to come to you on the water." Come," He said. Then Peter got out of the boat, walked on the water and came toward Jesus. But when he saw the wind, he was afraid, and, beginning to sink, cried out, "Lord, save me!" Immediately Jesus reached out His hand and caught him. "You of little faith," He said, "why did you doubt?" (Matthew 14:25-31)

When we, like Peter, do not recognize Jesus' power to work out solutions to problems, we can become terrified, too. Peter's trust in Christ enabled him to begin walking to meet Christ on the water. But the strong wind whipped up the sea and frightened Peter into doubting Christ's sufficiency for him. Isn't this what happens to us sometimes? When problems or anticipated problems threaten, we can begin to fear for ourselves and our loved ones. We fear that we'll have to face demands we aren't strong enough to meet. It is true that apart from Christ we can do nothing (see John 15:5). Yet we can each say with Paul, *"I can do everything through Him* [Christ] *who gives me strength"* (Phil. 4:13).

In fact, God commanded us not to fear and promised to give us victory regardless of the situation.

"So do not fear, for I am with you; do not be dismayed, for I am your God. I will strengthen you and help you; I will uphold you with My right hand" (Isaiah 41:10).

Jesus also lovingly reminded us of our heavenly Father's watchful care.

Are not two sparrows sold for a penny? Yet not one of them will fall to the ground apart from the will of your Father. And even the very hairs of your head are all numbered. So don't be afraid; you are worth more than many sparrows (Matthew 10:29-31).

We must recognize the deadly trap of fear set for us by satan and claim Psalm 27:1: *"The Lord is my light and my salvation—whom shall I fear? The Lord is the stronghold of my life—of whom shall I be afraid?"*

DEPRESSION

Another deadly trap that can ruin your beauty is mental depression, which is a major problem today. Depression can be caused by an abnormal physical or spiritual condition. You can become depressed because of an imbalance in your body chemistry or other physical malfunctions. If you think you are depressed, consult a doctor. If he or she determines that the cause of your depression is physical, he or she will undoubtedly discuss with you some of the many available treatment plans.

A violation of God's principles can also cause depression. Whereas living by His principles produces an abundant life, violating these principles results in a defeated one. Through the prophet Jeremiah, God said, *"Your own conduct and actions have brought this* [disaster] *upon you. This is your punishment. How bitter it is! How it pierces to the heart"* (Jer. 4:18). The Lord reminded Cain of this principle just before he murdered his brother Abel.

The Lord said to Cain, "Why are you angry? Why is your face downcast? If you do what is right, will you not be accepted? But if you do not do what is right, sin is crouching at your door; it desires to have you, but you must master it" (Genesis 4:6-7).

If we allow anger, fear, or self-pity to exist unchecked in our lives, depression can result.

We can each avoid depression (assuming it is not the result of a physical problem) by focusing our thoughts on our position in Christ rather than on conditions around us.

Since, then, you have been raised with Christ, set your hearts on things above, where Christ is seated at the right hand of God. Set your minds on things above, not on earthly things. For [as far as this world is concerned] *you died, and your life is now hidden with Christ in God* (Colossians 3:1-3).

Our position in union with Christ is the basis of all our spiritual life and growth. This position was established for eternity, and it is ours when we receive Jesus Christ as our personal Savior. *"Therefore if anyone is in Christ, he is a new creation..."* (2 Cor. 5:17).

At the moment of our salvation, we each obtain a permanent relationship with God that guarantees, among other things, that we will live with God forever. Christ paid for all our sins. We have the life of Christ (eternal life), and we share the righteousness and destiny of Christ. In other words, we Christians are the beneficiaries of an inheritance as heirs of God and joint heirs with Christ. Concentrating on our privileged status in Christ is like drawing on a million dollars that a benefactor has deposited in our bank accounts. Concentrating on unpleasant conditions is like living in poverty, unaware of those available riches.

The principle of focusing on our position in Christ can be illustrated in the following way. A roomful of women will have their minds on various details of life. One might be thinking about her neighbor. Another might be thinking about a point of conversation. But when a celebrity walks in, all of the women will focus their attention on her. Likewise, we are to focus our lives and attention on Jesus Christ and our position in Him. Then, the details of life will fall into place, and we will begin to enjoy the inheritance that is already ours.

The next time when you are angry, fearful, or depressed, ask the Lord to show you what you are angry about, what you are fearful of, or why you are depressed. As He gives you insights, you may remember what incident transpired, setting those feelings into motion. Ask Him to heal these places from within and give you wisdom in applying the new revelation. His delight is to heal that which He exposes.

A Peaceful Spirit Leads to Domestic Tranquility

God is orderly and wants you and your husband to have a peaceful life. *"For God is not a God of disorder but of peace....But everything should be done in a fitting and orderly way"* (1 Cor. 14:33,40).

In order to develop a peaceful spirit and a tranquil, orderly household, you will need to plan, organize, and exercise self-discipline. If you feel you can't handle a home and family in an orderly manner, ask for God's help. If you are His child, you can go directly to Him in Jesus' name. *"Let us then approach the throne of grace with confidence, so that we may receive mercy and find grace to help us in our time of need"* (Heb. 4:16). God promises to help each of us use our time wisely when we trust Him. *"Reverence for God adds hours to each day; so how can the wicked expect a long, good life?..."* (Prov. 10:27 TLB). *"I, Wisdom, will make the hours of your day more profitable and the years of your life more fruitful"* (Prov. 9:11 TLB).

> God is orderly and wants you
> and your husband to have
> a peaceful life.

When we are organized and purposeful in our lifestyles, Christ is honored.

> *Be very careful, then, how you live—not as unwise but as wise, making the most of every opportunity, because the days are evil. Therefore do not be foolish, but understand what the Lord's will is* (Ephesians 5:15-17).

Our ministry in our homes can be exciting, creative adventures. And most important, if Christ is controlling our lives, we are serving Him as we care for our families.

One way to get organized is to design a flexible plan by which you can accomplish your responsibilities. Then look to God for help. *"We should make plans—counting on God to direct us"* (Prov. 16:9 TLB). *"Commit your work to God so it will succeed"* (Prov. 16:3 TLB). Keep in mind your priorities: (1) personal relationship with Jesus Christ; (2) husband; (3) children; (4) personal grooming and rest; (5) household responsibilities; (6) outside ministry. Before you schedule your daily activities, consider how the following list (or a similar one) might be helpful in keeping your priorities in order:

1. Time with the Lord (studying His Word, soaking in His presence, and prayer)

2. Your responsibilities outside the home, such as an occupation

3. Time with your husband

4. Individual time with child(ren)

5. Collective time with your family

6. Meals, dishes, and housework

7. Individual hobbies, interests, and activities

8. Time to rest and relax

9. Outside ministry (church, meetings with other women, etc.)

10. Given responsibilities (shopping, paying bills, correspondence, etc.)

Following are a few tips for your consideration:

⚘ Start each day by making a list of what you have to do. Then work out a reasonable schedule for getting them done. You may have to cut out some TV, unnecessary shopping, or long phone conversations. You may have to learn to say no to good activities that are not essential. But if you know what your priorities are, you will not sacrifice the best for something that is merely good. You owe your husband your best, whether it's your attention, appearance, or providing a tranquil household.

⚘ Practice multi-tasking when appropriate.

⚘ Save steps by placing items that go to the basement near the basement door. Make one trip at the end of the day rather than several during the day unless you want the exercise.

- ೫ Have a long cord on your kitchen phone (or buy a cordless phone or hands-free headset) so you can cook, clean your kitchen, dust, or fold clothes while talking on the phone.

- ೫ As you drive, listen to Bible-study CDs that help you grow spiritually.

- ೫ If you have a child, take the necessary time to train him or her to care for clothing, toys, personal appearance, and so forth. It may seem easier to do the work yourself at first, but once your child is properly trained, his or her help will save you time. Besides, part of your job is to train your children to be more self-reliant and responsible.

- ೫ Plan ahead and build in flexibility for the unexpected. Again, the wise woman of Proverbs 31 is a good example: *"When it snows, she has no fear for her household; for all of them are clothed in scarlet"* (Prov. 31:21).

- ೫ Discover new and different ways to serve food. "Variety is the spice of cooking." Avoid preparing the same thing each week. Add new dishes that friends recommend or that look good in your cookbook. If your husband's likes are limited, try to fix the foods he likes as tastily as possible. And keep your child(ren)'s likes and dislikes in mind, too.

- ೫ When you prepare a favorite dish of the family, try doubling the recipe and freezing half for unexpected company or for a quick family meal.

⊚ Recognize your influence. Not only do you have inexhaustible opportunities to support and complement your husband, you may be helping to train children whose lives will affect hundreds of other lives.

As God enables you to develop various skills, you will find that in your home you are a teacher, nurse, interior decorator, manager, dietitian, seamstress, purchasing agent, counselor, consultant, photographer...you name it. What greater challenge could any woman want? We have heard the saying that necessity is a great teacher. That is true for me. When I was teaching mathematics in high school and pregnant with our first son, I needed maternity clothes. We had very little money to spend and I knew the only way was to make my outfits. By being very careful and following the instructions I was able to produce the outfits that I needed. This ignited a desire to sew which served me well for many years. Later, the furniture we had was much worn but there was not money to replace the chairs and sofa. I once again launched out into the unknown to see if I could reupholster them using some material purchase on sale. Yes, it worked. I knew it wasn't professional, but it worked for us and my self-esteem was strengthened. When God showed me this book was to be written, it meant developing one of my greatest areas of weakness. I made good grades in college except for composition. With complete dependency upon my Lord and cooperation with helpful friends, His strength came through in my weakness. I love cooperating with God and watching as He develops new areas of my life. Let Him challenge your weak areas and watch His power show up to bless you. You will find your portfolio expanding.

The final key to timeless beauty is walking in God's presence, living our lives before Him as an audience of One! His presence is what transforms our lives, as Second Corinthians states.

"But we all, with unveiled face, beholding as in a mirror the glory of the Lord, are being transformed into the same image from glory to glory, just as by the Spirit of the Lord" (2 Corinthians 5:7 NASB).

We walk in His presence by faith knowing that as we draw near to God He draws near to us (see 2 Cor. 5:7; James 4:8).

Endnote

1. Leaf, Dr. Caroline *Who Switched Off My Brain?* (Nashville TN: Thomas Nelson Publishers, 2009), 5.

10

How to Handle Problems and Trials

No matter where we live, how hard we try, or which self-help books we read, problems and trials come our way. We make mistakes and face not only the consequences of our actions, but those of other people—including our husbands.

OUR PROBLEMS AND TRIALS

Although we can't control everything that happens to us, we can choose how we will respond to what happens. Fortunately God has provided us with everything we believers need—including the Bible and the Holy Spirit—to face and overcome tough challenges. Let's explore a few of them now.

MISTAKES

Millie reaped great dividends when she applied the principle found in Proverbs 28:13: *"A man [or woman] who refuses to admit his mistakes can never be successful. But if he confesses and forsakes them, he gets another chance"* (TLB). During a hurried afternoon of juggling children's schedules and activities, she locked her keys in the car. Her husband, Ralph, had the only other key, so she had to call him at work. He had not been sympathetic to her previous blunders and didn't sound happy this time. "I'm sorry for the inconvenience this will cause you after such a hard day's work," Millie told him. "We'll wait here for you until you can come get us."

When Ralph arrived, he seemed pleased with his wife's response and calm spirit. Instead of fussing at her, he rewarded her by taking the family out to dinner.

Don't be disappointed if your husband does not respond positively to your mistakes as quickly as Ralph did. You may have to patiently and lovingly win back your man's approval over a period of time. If your mistake involves sin, be comforted by the fact that God will forgive you immediately even if your husband has not yet learned to do so. Your peace will come from knowing you are living according to God's will through His Word.

What about the mistakes your husband makes? The Bible addresses this aspect of life, too. *"Love forgets mistakes; nagging about them parts the best of friends"* (Prov. 17:9 TLB). His mistakes will not be corrected by mistaken behavior on your part. *"Don't repay evil for evil. Wait for the Lord to handle the matter"* (Prov. 20:22 TLB).

PERSONAL CRITICISM

How should you respond to criticism from your husband? *"It is a badge of honor to accept valid criticism"* (Prov. 25:12 TLB). *"Don't refuse to accept criticism; get all the help you can* (Prov. 23:12 TLB). *"The man* [or woman] *who is often reproved but refuses to accept criticism will suddenly be broken and never have another chance"* (Prov. 29:1 TLB). Receive your husband's criticism as a reminder from the Lord to investigate your actions and make proper adjustments. Remember, God holds him responsible for his household and may be using him to correct mistakes in your home.

> If you maintain a sweet, gentle spirit by drawing on Christ's power within you, God will use even invalid criticism to develop your inner spiritual qualities.

Sometimes you may receive criticism that you feel is not valid. However, if you maintain a sweet, gentle spirit by drawing on Christ's power within you, God will use even invalid criticism to develop your inner spiritual qualities.

STRIFE

Regardless of what causes strife between us and our husbands (pride, anger, contentious questions, and so forth), the Bible condemns it and offers powerful and effective solutions to help us deal with it. *"It is to a man's honor to avoid strife,"* Proverbs 20:3 reads, *"but every fool is quick to quarrel."* Paul, in Romans 1:29, took strife so seriously that he listed it with other serious sins: *"envy, murder, strife, deceit and malice."*

> Strife is easiest dealt with before it gets out of control.

Just as Matthew 5:25 urges us to come to terms quickly with an accuser, we are to seek reconciliation with our husbands. Strife is easiest dealt with before it gets out of control. *"It is hard to stop a quarrel once it starts, so don't let it begin"* (Prov. 17:14 TLB). When fighting is allowed to continue, strong walls are built up that are difficult to remove.

> *"It is harder to win back the friendship of an offended brother* [or spouse] *than to capture a fortified city. His anger shuts you out like iron bars"* (Proverbs 18:19 TLB).

We may have to confront our pride. We may have to seek forgiveness for things we have done. We may have to forgive even when our husbands haven't apologized. Whenever strife arises, face it quickly! Ask God to help you root out any sin in your life that is a factor in causing it. And by all means, we must not allow our hurt feelings to stand in the way of making the first move in correcting an unpleasant situation. God often uses the one who is most sensitive to His Spirit to bring health into a situation.

I had the opportunity to apply these principles shortly after learning them. My busy schedule was keeping me from my household responsibilities. One morning at breakfast, DeWitt pointed this out to me after asking me when I was going to mend the pants he had given me weeks earlier. I realized I was not as efficient a wife as I wanted to be and felt hurt. Instead of responding in a less-than-loving way, I let the Holy Spirit ease my pain and managed to say, "I'm sorry I didn't mend them earlier, DeWitt. Thanks for helping me get my priorities straight."

Since this was a new response on my part, he was as shocked as I was to hear it. After a moment of silence, he said, "Oh, that's all right. I was just feeling grouchy this morning and took it out on you." You see, he reacted kindly because I responded properly and promptly rather than attempting to justify or excuse my actions.

What about unkind remarks your husband makes to you or about you? First, realize that he may be teasing you, not knowing how much he is hurting you by what he considers to be innocent comments. Many times we get hurt unnecessarily because we don't understand our husbands. Your husband's unpleasant actions or attitudes may not necessarily be a personal attack on you. Realize that business, physical, or emotional pressures may be influencing his reactions. You owe it to him and yourself, though, to tell him how you feel about what he says. He is not a mind reader; you cannot understand each other without communication. Help him by sympathizing rather than adding to his problems by pouting, fussing, or whatever you do destructively when you are hurt or offended.

To ensure the best communication possible, choose a time to discuss this when your relationship is good and your husband seems to be in an understanding mood. Be sure that your words and attitudes are loving and in no way violate other principles (like trying to get him to change or making him feel guilty). Speak the truth in love (see Eph. 4:15). *"A gentle answer turns away wrath, but a harsh word stirs up anger"* (Prov. 15:1). This is the only response that will be effective and reap the desired results. *"Through patience a ruler can be persuaded, and a gentle tongue can break a bone"* (Prov. 25:15). Keep in mind, however, that ultimately it is God's job to deal with him concerning his problem, not yours.

Responding in love does not mean
that you are to be a doormat
or have an apathetic or passive attitude.

Remember, responding in love does not mean that you are to be a doormat or have an apathetic or passive attitude. You may express love in many ways. You may express it forcefully, but never with a condemning or martyr-like attitude. You should also be realistic. If you have absurd, overly sweet reactions to your husband's indiscreet remarks, you'll place yourself on a pedestal where your husband can't reach you, love you, and have a normal and real relationship with you.

One woman I know communicates her feelings to her husband through exaggerated words and actions. When her husband says something she doesn't like, she playfully sticks out her tongue or lower lip at him. When he ignores her, she says in mock self-pity something like, "I'm going out to eat green worms till I die. Then you'll be sorry!" Through such antics, she lets her husband know how she feels without getting angry. Her husband knows she has spunk, is fascinated by her, and is learning to be more careful of his words, attitudes, and actions.

If your husband does not refrain from making unkind comments after you have expressed your feelings, you can apply the principle in Proverbs 10:12: *"Hatred stirs up dissension, but love covers over all wrongs."* If you trust Christ to give you a forgiving attitude, He will build strong character in you and guide you in responding to your husband. You might also seek out a wise, godly counselor who can provide a listening ear and appropriate help.

SINFUL ATTITUDES

What should your response be to sinful mental attitudes (pride, jealousy, bitterness, vindictiveness, implacability, guilt complex, hatred, worry, anger, and fear) in the lives of other people, especially your husband? As always, God has an answer. *"Do not answer a fool according to his folly, or you will be like him yourself"* (Prov. 26:4). (The word translated *folly* here refers to sins of mental attitude.)

If your husband is controlled by a sinful attitude such as bitterness and you become involved emotionally with his problem, you too can be overcome by sinful emotions. As much as possible, your involvement should be limited and non-emotional. Allow God to deal directly with your husband, convicting or disciplining him as necessary. If you have not gotten emotionally involved, any animosity your husband expresses will be between him and God. *"Do not take revenge my friends, but leave room for God's wrath, for it is written: 'It is Mine to avenge; I will repay,' says the Lord"* (Rom. 12:19).

Perhaps you are thinking, *My husband is so gross in his attitudes and actions that I cannot respect and reverence him as Ephesians 5:33 commands. What do I do about obeying this command?* The Christian life is a life of faith, trusting Christ to be who and what He claims to be (see Heb. 11:1,6). You can be sure that what God tells you to do, He is willing to perform through you. If you follow the principle of reverencing and responding to your husband by faith, your actions will demonstrate love, respect, and reverence even though you do not feel those emotions. God is faithful and will, according to your need, reward your obedience to His requirements.

PRAISE OR LACK OF PRAISE

Many women have said to me, in effect, "My husband does not admire and praise me as he does others.

How can I get him to?" God offers this wisdom: *"It is not good to eat too much honey, nor is it honorable to seek one's own honor"* (Prov. 25:27). If you seek or demand your husband's praise, you'll cause trouble and hurt feelings.

You will attain praise and glory by focusing on Jesus Christ, His Word, and His will for your life. As you do this, He will provide you with praise and honor at the right time. When you are content with only Jesus' approval, your husband's praise will be a pleasant reward rather than a necessity.

> *"Let love and faithfulness never leave you; bind them around your neck, write them on the tablet of your heart. Then you will win favor and a good name in the sight of God and man"* (Proverbs 3:3-4).

As God's Word fills and controls your heart and mind, you will gain the praise of your man. Wait for it; do not demand it.

How should you, in contrast, respond to praise from your husband or others? *"The crucible for silver and the furnace for gold, but a man* [or woman] *is tested by the praise he receives"* (Prov. 27:21). You will not have a problem with pride if you are aware that you are simply a vessel God uses to do His good work. The most gracious way to respond to a compliment or praise is with a simple "thank you," reflecting a grateful heart.

OVER-CONCERN WITH OTHERS' OPINIONS

Comparing yourself to other women or fearing that other people will not accept you as you are will always create problems. Do not spoil your beauty by focusing on other people and allowing them to govern your attitudes, actions, and responses. Describing people who did this, the apostle Paul wrote, *"...When they measure themselves by themselves and compare themselves with themselves, they are not wise"* (2 Cor. 10:12). It is easy to think, *If I were like Sue, my husband would like me better.* It never helps, however, to try to copy another person's dress, mannerisms, or personality. Your husband chose to marry you because you were the one he loved. You can pick up beauty hints or other tips from other people, but do not try to be a carbon copy of anyone else.

> Your husband chose
> to marry you because you were
> the one he loved.

Proverbs 29:25 addresses the fear of not being accepted: *"Fear of man will prove to be a snare, but whoever trusts in the Lord is kept safe."* Fear is not from the Lord. *"For God did not give us a spirit of timidity, but a spirit of power, of love and of self-discipline"* (2 Tim. 1:7).

Being overly concerned about other people's reactions to your husband's behavior can also create problems between the two of you. You will know if you are overly concerned if you find yourself correcting your husband based on others' opinions, seeking to clarify his actions or comments by further explanation, or apologizing to others for his behavior. He will take your comments as an indication that you do not trust his ability to handle a situation or make a favorable impression on others. He'll feel that you are not accepting him as he is and are attempting to be a go-between in his relationships with others. And he will be right.

If your husband has not made himself clear or has been misunderstood, let him work out the problem. Only then will he gain self-confidence and improve his ability to communicate clearly and interact with others appropriately. It is your responsibility to encourage and comfort him, not to mother him, correct him, or improve him. You can avoid needless frustration and tension if you ask yourself, *Am I assuming responsibility that is not mine as his wife?* Many frustrations and tensions come when you assume responsibility that is not yours. I'd add these clarifications, though. Sometimes it is appropriate to bring up a way in which your husband has miscommunicated or even offended someone, but do it in love. Also, if your husband's behavior is clearly sinful, there are times when you need to bring this to his attention, even if it means confronting him lovingly.

SMALL IRRITATIONS

Your inner beauty will be apparent if you learn to take even small irritations in stride and allow Christ to use them to make you lovelier. One day, June was in a big hurry and spilled milk in the backseat of the car. Instead of panicking or getting angry at herself, she asked God what He wanted to teach her through this irritation. He immediately reminded her that she needed to slow down. When she shared this thought with her husband, he said, "You're beautiful on the inside and the outside!"

No matter what may be causing you unrest, disharmony, or confusion, God has set forth a principle in his Word through which you can gain harmony and peace. Ask yourself, *Can the problem that is causing distress be corrected or removed?* Even as you can oil a squeaky hinge on a door, you can correct many problems. Trust God to use the difficulties to mold you into His image.

The Importance of Faith During Trials

Faith is another word for believing that what God says in His Word is true even though you have no visible proof. The Christian life is a life of faith (see 2 Cor. 5:7). You take many steps by faith, you receive Christ by faith, you are forgiven of your sins by faith, you are controlled by the Holy Spirit by faith, and you face trials by faith, yet the results are not based on the amount of faith you have, but on the object of your faith—Jesus Christ.

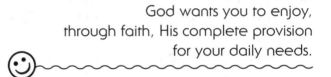

God wants you to enjoy,
through faith, His complete provision
for your daily needs.

God wants you to enjoy, through faith, His complete provision for your daily needs. And it is wonderful to know that at the moment you receive Christ, you receive, potentially, all He can give you to meet those needs: *"Praise be to the God and Father of our Lord Jesus Christ, who has blessed us in the heavenly realms with every spiritual blessing in Christ"* (Eph. 1:3).

When times are difficult, you are to ask Jesus how to appropriate what He has already provided for you on the cross. As you seek Him, He may use the Word, others, circumstances, or other means to speak to your heart and make His truth come alive. Then apply it by faith. (See Colossians 2:3.)

Any decision you make must always be based on the solid, unchangeable facts in God's Word rather than on how you feel. Moods and emotions come and go, but God's Word never changes. Sometimes your feelings will motivate and encourage you, but other times they will pull you down. So, your feelings should never be the basis for your actions—and this is especially true during difficult times. Your decisions must be based on truths about God's character and His Word, and it will no doubt encourage you to also look at what He has done for you and others. A life of faith in Christ will not always be easy, but it is the only life that offers incorruptible beauty whatever happens in life.

As we think about the relationship between our faith and our obedience and how challenging it can be to maintain faith during difficult times, let's look at what God taught Moses so many years ago, as recorded in Exodus 4.

> *Then the Lord said to him, "What is that in your hand?"*
> *"A staff," he replied.*
> *The Lord said, "Throw it on the ground."*
> *Moses threw it on the ground and it became a snake, and he ran from it* (Exodus 4:2-3)

Moses' rod was familiar and useful to him in his responsibilities as a shepherd. He had no reason to throw it down before God except in obedience. Moses trusted and obeyed God on the basis of God's words alone, not because the request seemed sensible. Once Moses obeyed and threw down his staff, it became a snake.

"Then the Lord said to him, 'Reach out your hand and take it by the tail'..." (Exod. 4:4). Moses could have responded by saying, "But what about the head, Lord?

I'm frightened!" Instead, Moses again trusted God. *"... So Moses reached out and took hold of the snake and it turned back into a staff in his hand"* (Exod. 4:4).

Likewise, when we fulfill our responsibility by obeying and trusting the Lord, we can be confident that He will work out each detail of a situation for our ultimate benefit. Moses' rod was returned to him, but the snake (representing any harmful ingredient) was removed.

Now I'd like to get very personal with you. Do you hesitate to surrender some facet of your life to the Lord? Could it be that you are unwilling to totally trust Him with your husband, children, career, possessions, or difficult situations? You, too, can accept and experience God's complete provision for you, through faith, by surrendering each area of your life to Christ, knowing that if He returns it to you, it will be purified and safe for your enjoyment. When you surrender areas of your life to Him, you do not lose anything; you gain fulfillment. You can trust Him!

Another way you can accept God's complete provision for you through faith is by thanking God for everything in your life, including the problems and trials. The apostle Paul wrote, *"Give thanks in **all** circumstances, for this is God's will for you in Christ Jesus"* (1 Thess. 5:18). Thanking God for *everything* in your life shows that you believe God's Word. He promises that even though everything in our lives is not good, He will work out all things for our good as we trust Him (see Rom. 8:28).

Is this concept new to you? I learned years ago that I should give thanks in all things, but I did not apply this principle in my life for a long time. I was in the habit of thanking God for things in my life that I knew were good and that I could understand, but I never thanked

Him for unpleasant situations. Finally I decided to give thanks in all situations.

One morning, my decision was tested severely. A heavy ice storm had covered the Atlanta area when De-Witt left for work. Later in the morning, his office called to see if he would be coming in. I told them he had left about two hours earlier. The gentleman replied, "Since it only takes him about 30 minutes to drive to work, I guess he had an accident on the icy expressway."

At that point, I had the choice of trusting and thanking God or giving way to hysterical fear. Knowing that God loved DeWitt more than I did, that He is sovereign, and that He promises not to allow anything to happen to His children without working it out to their ultimate benefit, I said, "Thank You, Lord, for whatever situation DeWitt is in."

God honored my obedience to His Word by giving me peace. Jesus said, *"Peace I leave with you; My peace I give to you. I do not give to you as the world gives. Do not let your hearts be troubled and do not be afraid"* (John 14:27). The peace God gave me did not hinge on DeWitt's circumstances. As it turned out, DeWitt was delayed because of other accidents, not his own.

I encourage you to apply this principle of giving thanks in all situations, especially to minor incidents in daily life such as dropping an egg on your freshly cleaned floor, an inconvenient telephone call, or an unappreciative husband. As you learn to be thankful during the small problems in your life, you will find it more natural to be thankful during larger trials and crises. Of course, you can rejoice only when you focus on God's provision, His sovereign control, and His ability to work everything out for your ultimate good.

Because of His sufficiency, you can live above your circumstances instead of under them, and life will take on a new, wonderful dimension. With a thankful heart, you will experience real joy.

You see, your joy will not depend on circumstances, but on your relationship and fellowship with God. If you only choose to react to circumstances and people around you, you will be happy when circumstances and other people are pleasant, but sad when they are unpleasant. In other words, reacting to conditions around you produces an unstable existence. But if you reflect on Jesus Christ and hold fast to God's Word, you can have peace and stability whether or not you get the outfit you want or have to live with a grouchy husband. Accept the victory Christ promises you in John 16:33: *"I have told you these things, so that in Me you may have peace. In this world you will have trouble. But take heart! I have overcome the world."*

Even though you surrender your life to Christ, He will not assume responsibilities He has assigned to you.

Realize, however, that even though you surrender your life to Christ, He will not assume responsibilities He has assigned to you. For example, He will not make decisions for you or open your mouth so you will share His truth with someone else. But He will empower you once you make a Spirit-inspired decision and, in faith, act on it.

When I first understood that Christ desired to live in and through me (see Gal. 2:20), I excitedly shared his desire with my then 3-year-old son. "Isn't it good news, Ken, that we can trust Christ to live through us rather than trying to do it ourselves?"

"Yes," he answered, "that's good."

Later, when I told him to pick up his toys, he said, "Let Jesus do it. I don't have to."

I then reminded him that Jesus would live His life through him by using his arms and legs to pick up toys.

"Oh, is that how it works?" he asked.

Christ will not make your decisions for you. He expects you to make them on the basis of His Word as led by His Spirit. Then He will provide the power you need to carry them out, no matter how challenging or difficult your life or marriage may be.

11

Reviewing Beauty Basics

J esus Christ, the divine artist at work in you, creates real, fadeless inner beauty, as I explained in Chapter 9. Your inner self (the living canvas) will become radiantly beautiful under His workmanship. Your body (the picture frame) complements or enhances the painting. Both the canvas and frame, however, must be as attractive as possible so people will enjoy the painting. Whereas an unattractive or inappropriate frame can detract from a good painting, a wisely chosen frame will add that extra touch that can make even an ordinary picture look beautiful.

> Whereas an unattractive or inappropriate frame can detract from a good painting, a wisely chosen frame will add that extra touch that can make even an ordinary picture look beautiful.

It should encourage you to know that both your body (picture frame) and your inner self (canvas) are precious to God.

"May God Himself, the God of peace, sanctify you through and through. May your whole spirit, soul and

body be kept blameless at the coming of our Lord Jesus Christ" (1 Thessalonians 5:23).

The apostle Paul wrote,

"Do you not know that your body is a temple of the Holy Spirit?...You are not your own; you were bought at a price. Therefore honor God with your body" (1 Corinthians 6:19-20).

God considers your body to be important, and you should, too.

Your body is like a palace where royalty lives! You will want it to be glorious and beautiful, shining and polished, to honor the King of kings. The psalmist expressed the desire that *"our daughters will be like pillars carved to adorn a palace"* (Ps. 144:12).

A pleasing, socially acceptable appearance gives you a wider witness for Christ and increases your effectiveness. Good grooming is looking your best for Him, not drawing attention to yourself. Your overall appearance should be the best you can accomplish within your budget and should be in keeping with your role and position.

If you are a Christian, everything you do and are, and even the way you look, reflects on your Savior as well as yourself. So it is doubly important that you be well groomed. *"Whatever you do, do it all for the glory of God"* (1 Cor. 10:31). Try to make your body as attractive as possible. People form ideas about the "real you" by the outward clues you furnish. They accept you, in part, on the basis of your self-appraisal, which is often expressed in your grooming.

Your appearance should reflect self-respect and self-esteem. When you are not well-groomed, it is as if you are saying, "I consider myself unworthy of care. I don't think I'm valuable enough to spend time on." Yet when you remember that God considers your body to be important, that your looks reflect on your Savior, and that you are a child of God purchased by the blood of Jesus Christ (see 1 Cor. 7:23; Eph. 1:7), you can't help but rejoice and realize that you are a person of worth.

Some well-meaning people still believe that we are not spiritual when we are well groomed. They use First Peter 3:3 to say that we should not care for our hair, wear jewelry, or dress attractively. This verse reads, *"Whose adorning let it not be that outward adorning of plaiting the hair, and of wearing of gold, or of putting on of apparel"*(1 Pet. 3:3 KJV). Such people always stop in their reasoning before they finish the verse; otherwise they would have to conclude that we are not to put on clothing! Our spirituality is determined by whether or not Christ is controlling our lives, not by what we try to do to make ourselves seem spiritual.

As we've seen, your role as a wife involves developing a relationship with your husband that will bring joy to both of you. Just as a career involves spending time updating your skills so you will be successful in your field, your identity as a woman requires you to spend time making and keeping yourself attractive. When Ruth was preparing to win her husband-to-be, for example, Naomi told her, *"Wash and perfume yourself, and put on your best clothes. Then go..."* (Ruth 3:3). Of course you should not spend all your time, thought, and money on your appearance, but take some time to make yourself as lovely as possible.

A REVIEW OF GOOD GROOMING

Cleanliness

Perhaps it goes without saying, but one important way to be lovely is to be sure your body is as clean as possible. It has been said that "cleanliness is next to godliness." Reverence for God should produce reverence for your body. Bathing regularly will help you to stay clean and to feel feminine. (Of course, your freshness will last longer if you use a good deodorant.)

You may want to choose your favorite fragrance as a delightful finishing touch to your daily routine. Find a cologne or perfume that appeals to your husband and make it your "signature" scent. Every time he smells it then, it will remind him of you.

Diet

Are you aware that what goes on inside you shows up on the outside? Providing a healthy body for the Holy Spirit to live in requires self-discipline. If you want to maintain a healthy weight, you must prepare wholesome, nourishing, well-balanced meals for yourself and your family. If you have gained a few extra pounds, it is important to your health, your self-image, and your husband to lose them. But consult a doctor before trying a strict or extreme diet. Be careful that you are not trying to duplicate an image that Hollywood presents of a perfect female body. Rather, know that each of us is unique and has our own special beauty. Here is where your doctor can help you have a healthy perspective.

You can take sensible precautions against eating too many calories by cutting down on between-meal snacks, heavy pastries, rich desserts, and carbonated drinks. Drink plenty of water. You do not have to stop eating. Just train your taste buds to enjoy nonfattening, nourishing foods. Generally speaking, when you eat moderate portions of nourishing food and get enough exercise, your weight will not fluctuate much. Years ago I chose to eat more nutritional foods as a way of life. At that time I found it easy to maintain the weight I desired by simply eliminating sugar and carbonated drinks. However, today I have to work harder by cutting down portions, eating less carbohydrates, and adding more exercise. Find out how many calories you need to maintain your correct weight and eat accordingly. Many excellent books address proper nutrition and diet.

Exercise

If you don't get enough exercise, you will feel sluggish, gain weight, and/or get flabby. Be sure to exercise regularly each week, outdoors if possible. Join a health club; ride a bicycle; work in the yard; take long walks. Whatever you do, you will find that proper exercise will increase your flexibility, give you more energy each day, give you a firmer figure, and generate more enthusiasm for life. My favorite ways of exercising are riding my bicycle outside or a stationary bicycle inside, jumping on my trampoline, or walking. I must confess that I not only need to devote more energy to being as consistent as I know that I should, but also to not take the easy way out. The easy way out would be to place a block on the floor in the center of the room, walk around the block twice, sit down and relax. If anyone asks me if I have exercised today, then I tell them that I have walked around the block twice!

Rest

An active wife also needs time to rest and relax. If you are also a mother with small children, you may be able to rest only while they are taking naps. Regardless of when you do it, take time to relax and do not feel guilty about it. Jesus told His disciples to *"come with Me by yourselves to a quiet place and get some rest"* (Mark 6:31). If the Son of God recognized the need for relaxation, you should, too. It will help you stay more fresh and alert as you fulfill your many responsibilities.

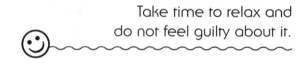

Take time to relax and do not feel guilty about it.

Makeup

Proper skin care and makeup are important in achieving and maintaining a lovely complexion. Most cosmetic studios or large department stores have skin-care and makeup analysts who will serve you without charge. Make use of their free services. They will give you tips on how to apply makeup for your best look. Remember, when makeup is skillfully applied, other people will be aware of your loveliness, not your cosmetics.

Mannerisms

Watch yourself in a mirror to see if you have any distracting facial mannerisms when you talk. Or ask a friend if she has noticed any. Do you chew or lick your lips unnecessarily? Do you grit your teeth or move your jaw from side to side? Make a conscious effort to correct such mannerisms, which will detract from your beauty.

Hair

Frame your face with a halo of beauty, your hair, which is a symbol of your femininity. One way your femininity contrasts with your husband's masculinity is through the care and style of your hair. Unkempt and unattractive hair does not glorify God or add to you.

Unkempt and unattractive hair does not glorify God or add to you.

The style of your hair should enhance the shape of your face. Consider current styles, but do not choose one just because it is fashionable. (It may not be right for you.) Experiment with your hair. Obtain the help of a professional. You might also ask your husband if he has an opinion.

Hands

As you consider ways to enhance your physical beauty, don't neglect your hands. Red, chapped hands prove that you wash dishes and floors, but don't care about the aftereffects. Ragged nails and cuticles reveal that you are a nervous chewer. Dirty nails suggest that you are not completely clean. Since neglected hands and nails spoil overall beauty, keep your hands as clean and soft as possible and your nails shaped and trimmed. This will not take too much time if you keep hand lotion, an emery board, and a pair of rubber gloves (for dirty work or washing) available.

Also, be sure you don't spoil the effect of lovely hands by restless, nervous, and fidgety actions. Nervous practices such as twisting your ring, gesturing, rubbing or stroking your chin, chewing your nails, or cracking your knuckles will mar your charm. Practice holding your hands in a graceful, relaxed position while you sit, stand, or talk.

Clothes

Carefully chosen clothes will add the final touches to your feminine appearance and please your husband. You can accentuate your good points and camouflage your bad points through the use of line, color, fabric, and pattern to make yourself look taller, shorter, fuller, or thinner. You can learn how to complement your figure by reading books or magazine articles or by shopping with a friend whose taste you admire and who will tell you what looks best on you. The Lord tells you to ask Him for wisdom. He'll help you express your own personality through your dress.

The wise woman described in Proverbs 31 dresses well: *"...She is clothed in fine linen..."* (Prov. 31:22). Following are a few tips to help you in your efforts to be well dressed:

- It is better to choose a few well-made, fashionable outfits than many poorly made garments.

- Explore local thrift stores and consignment shops. You will be amazed at the bargains you can find. (Remember, though, that a bargain is not a bargain unless you need and will wear what you buy.)

- ❧ Make your wardrobe appear larger by buying a few basic garments that you can vary through the use of scarves, belts, jewelry, vests, or mixing and matching.

- ❧ Determine which colors enhance your eye and skin color, and buy clothing with them in mind.

- ❧ Focus on proven styles, not just fashion fads that come and go.

- ❧ If you have time, add to your wardrobe inexpensively by sewing. If you do not know how to sew, you may be able to take an adult-education class or get instruction at a sewing center.

- ❧ Get ideas by browsing in fashionable clothing stores and noticing the trim, material, color combinations, and styles in use. Or look through catalogs or Websites.

Posture

No matter how well-groomed and well-dressed you are, you will ruin the whole effect if you slump, hunch, or swagger. Practice standing, walking, and sitting gracefully. Stand tall. Keep your feet together when you sit. As you walk, keep your feet parallel and your knees together.

Perhaps you're wondering why I just mentioned these "basics" when they seem so obvious. There are several reasons. First, I've met many women who do so well in applying the biblical principles we've explored so far, yet for various reasons ignore these "beauty basics." And, I've also discovered that sometimes we wives become so caught up in our daily responsibilities that we overlook key feminine details that play an important role in our own well-being, our marriages, and our overall physical, emotional, and spiritual health.

So, if you are already practicing these basics that will make you more attractive on the outside, thanks for bearing with me. And if you haven't yet managed to make each of these basics a priority, perhaps now you will be a bit more motivated to try.

Let's move now into the final chapter—one that's so important to all of us and is built on all the principles we've explored. Yes, it's the chapter on marital S-E-X.

12

Sexual Fulfillment in Your Marriage

G od's plans for you are perfect. There is no area in which He has not made total provision for your needs. Because He is interested in your complete personal fulfillment, God has provided a way in which you and your husband can experience and express the deep, intimate relationship He intends for you. One of those ways is through your sexual union.

SEX IS GOD'S IDEA!

God incorporated sexuality into His plan of creation.

The Lord God said, "It is not good for the man to be alone. I will make a helper suitable for him."…So God created man in His own image, in the image of God He created him; male and female He created them. God blessed them and said to them, "Be fruitful and increase in number; fill the earth and subdue it…" (Genesis 2:18; 1:27-28).

After God made Eve from Adam's rib, He gave her to Adam and said, *"A man will…be united to his wife, and they will become one flesh"* (Gen. 2:24). God instituted the marital relationship. The marriage of Adam and Eve set a pattern for humankind so that the human race could be perpetuated in maximum freedom, protection, and happiness. But more than that, God designed the sexual union of husband and wife to be an expression of love for each other. This union is described by the word translated "united," which means "to be joined" through a sexual relationship. God meant the sexual relationship to be a fulfilling, enjoyable part of the marriage. The Song of Solomon, as well as many other Scriptures, vividly describes the physical delight experienced during the union of married lovers (see Song of Sol. 6:1-10; 7:1-9).

MARITAL DELIGHTS

The physical union of you and your husband should be satisfying because it is an expression of your inner oneness. Being one in the soul means that your mind is filled with thoughts of your husband, you commit your will to giving him pleasure, and no one will ever take his place in your affections. Intercourse, then, becomes more than just a physical act since it portrays a much deeper soul relationship between you two.

God gives beautiful, positive instruction on how a couple's sexual needs are to be fulfilled through union in marriage. To the husband, Solomon wrote:

> *Drink water from your own cistern, running water from your own well....May your fountain be blessed, and may you rejoice in the wife of your youth. A loving doe, a graceful deer—may her breasts satisfy you always, may you ever be captivated by her love* (Proverbs 5:15, 18-19).

The beautiful parallel likens a person's thirst being satisfied by drinking cool, fresh water to a couple's sexual thirst being satisfied by regular intercourse.

Notice that God says to *"rejoice in the wife of your youth."* The sexual relationship is to provide both of you with great pleasure. You are described as graceful, loving, and satisfying. You are to concentrate on making your sex life a satisfying, fulfilling experience for your husband. Otherwise, how can your love *"captivate"* him? You should have great freedom and joy in satisfying your husband's sexual desires and needs, just as he should have the same freedom and joy in satisfying yours.

> You should have great freedom
> and joy in satisfying your
> husband's sexual desires and needs,
> just as he should have the same freedom
> and joy in satisfying yours.

Realizing that your husband needs the freedom to initiate sexual actions, communicate with him so you can better understand and meet one another's needs. Respond lovingly, being relaxed in the knowledge that it is God's will for you to meet his sexual needs enthusiastically. As you do, your mutual fulfillment and enjoyment will grow.

Mutual sexual fulfillment was not always a reality in Karen and Fred's life, but it is now. While growing up, Karen was not taught God's plan for sex. As a result, she had many preconceived notions when she got married. The sordid stories she had heard about marital sex caused her to think of her role in providing sex as an obligation or duty, which she dreaded. The books she read about sex did not release her from her warped ideas. Almost any techniques of lovemaking and sexual arousal left Karen burdened with a deep sense of guilt. She felt that such activities were perverted.

After hearing the lectures on which this book is based, Karen gained a different perspective on sexuality. Her eyes sparkled as she said to me, "I had no idea God had so much to say in his Word about sex. The Scriptures you mentioned showed me that sex is God's idea, not man's. It's designed to give pleasure to both my husband and me. I've learned to relax totally and enjoy the genuine desire we now have for each other."

PLAN AHEAD

As a wise wife, plan ahead in order to meet your husband's sexual needs. The following are some general tips:

- ⊛ Get the rest necessary in order to be alert, responsive, and available to your man. When you are tired or not particularly interested in sexual union, trust Jesus Christ to give you a new excitement and enthusiasm since it is His will for you both to receive sexual pleasure and fulfillment through your union. But also be honest. If you are dead tired, you may have good reason to postpone lovemaking.

- ⊛ Whenever possible, build some flexibility into your schedule so that you will be available to meet your husband's needs—at night, in the morning, or even in the middle of the day.

- ⊛ Sense when your husband is interested in lovemaking. Don't be like the wife who finds all sorts of things to do before going to bed or reads a magazine in bed until her husband turns over and forgets the whole thing. True, you can't be a mind reader, but be sensitive.

☺ Get to know your husband's sexual needs and desires.

Prepare yourself to make love by thinking positive thoughts that arouse you rather than negative ones that cause you to be irritated. If you fulfill your role as a wife by accepting your husband as he is, admiring him, making him the center of your life, and responding to his leadership, provision, and protection, you will not be giving him any reason for his eyes to wander to another woman. One of the main reasons for much unfaithfulness in marriage is emotional rather than sexual. Know more about your husband's needs and wants than any other woman. By acting on this knowledge, you will tip the scales significantly in your favor in preventing the seeds of infidelity from germinating.

> Know more about your husband's needs
> and wants than any other woman.

STRIVE FOR NEWNESS IN YOUR SEXUAL RELATIONSHIP

Do not ever let it be said of your marriage that the "newness" has worn off or that life has become dull and routine. Keep giving your marriage fresh spark by saying and doing unexpected things. For instance, after your husband comes home from work, whisper something in his ear like, "I'm in the mood; how about now?" Of course you may not literally expect him to take you up on your suggestion immediately since there may be children around and dinner to prepare. The thought, however, will stimulate him and remind him that he is desirable. This is just another way of saying, "I love you." As you make sex an exciting and meaningful part of your lives, your husband will not be tempted to feel that he is "missing out" or that the "newness" of marriage has worn off. He will look forward to the sexual and emotional gratification he has with you.

You are glorifying Jesus Christ when you think and plan toward being a good sexual partner for your husband. *"...A married woman is concerned about...how she can please her husband"* (1 Cor. 7:34). When you make sex an exciting and satisfying part of your life together, you will please your husband and be obedient to Christ's instructions to you. If you do not fulfill your husband's sexual needs, you may be a stumbling block in his life and cause him to be led away from spiritual truths instead of toward God. *"Do not deprive each other [sexually]...so that Satan will not tempt you because of your lack of self-control"* (1 Cor. 7:5).

> When you make sex an exciting and satisfying part of your life together, you will please your husband and be obedient to Christ's instructions to you.

Some men want their wives to read pornographic books or go to X-rated movies to see how they can add variety to their sex life. Show your husband that you can provide variety and excitement without such distorted "aids." Get ideas from some of the excellent Christian books on sex.[1] Feel free to "experiment" with your husband, trying some new things you both feel comfortable doing. Most of all, ask God to give you His ideas. They are always the best ones. As you do so, hopefully you will not have to address the distorted "aids." If you do, you might say something like, "Honey, I cannot participate in this activity. It would bring destruction to my inner being and damage my ability to respond to you with love and freedom."

You can also add freshness and variety to your marriage by making yourself beautiful, your bedroom irresistible, and your bed beautiful and comfortable. We read this description of the wise woman: *"She makes coverings for her bed..."* (Prov. 31:22).

Also, explore which of the following suggestions you might use to gradually add "newness" to your marriage. (Notice the word *gradually*. Your husband might be overwhelmed or even suspicious if you use all of these suggestions at once.)

1. Keep your bed clean and sweet smelling. If your husband likes perfume, spray a little of his favorite on the pillows or sheets. Satin sheets, fuzzy throws, and pillows can add a nice variety.

2. Use candlelight, soft light, or colored light to produce a romantic atmosphere in your bedroom. Millie said her husband had never been the "candlelight type." However, when she introduced candlelight to their bedroom, they both were thrilled with the effect.

3. Try playing soft music.

4. When circumstances permit, variety may be obtained by having sexual relations in different rooms, perhaps in front of a glowing fireplace. Be responsive and willing to have sex in a variety of positions, too.

5. If you have children at home, be sure you have privacy and a relaxed atmosphere. Lock your bedroom door if necessary.

6. Do not spoil the inviting scene you have created by wearing an old T-shirt or sleepwear that doesn't fit.

7. Use breath mints, spray, or mouthwash if needed. Something as simple as bad breath may keep your husband at a distance.

8. If possible, splurge on a new nightgown and dress attractively, drawing your husband's attention to your best features. Every woman has at least one good feature on which she can capitalize. It may be beautiful legs, shoulders, neck, breasts, or face. Make the most of what you have, and don't fret about what you do not have. Your most appealing outfit may be your "birthday suit." Never be embarrassed at being naked in front of your husband. Remember, your body belongs to him just as his belongs to you (see 1 Cor. 7:4).

9. Keep your husband aware of your femininity—the fact that you are an exciting woman and his lover. Exhibit your stimulating, challenging womanhood through your creativity. For instance, if you have children at home, arrange for them to spend a night or weekend with friends, and serve your husband's favorite meal by candlelight. Wear his favorite perfume, relax, and enjoy him.

10. Make your bedroom the most beautiful room in your home, since this is the room where you and your husband regularly display love

for each other. Always reserve this room for love—not for quarrels. However, a Christian couple may well come to God on their knees—in the bedroom—to ask His forgiveness for sharp words and wrong attitudes or for creativity in their sex life.

> Make your bedroom the most beautiful room in your home, since this is the room where you and your husband regularly display love for each other.

As you respond lovingly to your husband and fit into his plans according to God's order, you will see God perform amazing things in your marriage. When he is with you, your husband will feel complete and fulfilled because you are his counterpart—giving him what he does not have on his own. This beautiful relationship between you both can be focused in a sexual union in which your love and affection are expressed, increased, and fortified. Your sexual union creates a tender understanding, communion, and communication that cannot be expressed in language. As "one flesh," you will be able to do together what neither of you can do alone.

FACING SEX-RELATED PROBLEMS

Obviously there isn't room here to try to cover the myriad of sex-related problems that show up in various marriages. I do think, however, that it will be valuable to address a few key areas.

Regardless of your sexual needs or problems, remember that God promises to give wisdom to all who ask:

"If you want to know what God wants you to do, ask Him, and He will gladly tell you, for He is always ready to give a bountiful supply of wisdom to all who ask Him; He will not resent it" (James 1:5 TLB).

He may provide this wisdom through His Word, your pastor, another mature Christian, a Christian marriage and family counselor, or through information received from a book. The heavenly Father desires that your sex life be totally fulfilling for you and your husband.

If you and your spouse are experiencing sex-related problems, I encourage you to look for the sources so you can find permanent solutions. Since sex in marriage is an expression of the inner oneness of two people, it follows that problems can relate to any facet of either mate's life. Problems can be traced to such sources as spiritual issues, personality conflicts, misunderstandings, or abuse.

RECOGNIZE DIFFERENCES IN SEXUAL RESPONSE

Realizing how you and your husband differ sexually may help to correct some sexual problems. Generally, your husband will have a more aggressive, stronger sex drive than yours. This is understandable because God created the man to be the leader. Knowing this, you can find it easier to respond to his sexual leadership and expect complete satisfaction for both of you rather than being turned off by his sexual aggressiveness and need. Furthermore, a man is usually stimulated sexually by sight, but a woman normally is not. As your husband watches you undress for bed, he may become sufficiently aroused to be ready for intercourse while you are simply ready for bed.

Also, you and your husband may have different sexual responses after an argument. Your husband's way of saying, "I apologize for my behavior; now, let me show you how much I love you," may be to pursue sexual intercourse. But you may prefer to be reassured of his love with tender words and hugs before you are ready for sex. Furthermore, sex can serve as a tranquilizer for your husband, enabling him to relax and go to sleep. When you are tired, the last thing you may want is stimulating sex.

Realize, too, that your husband may believe that his masculinity is tied in with his ability to satisfy your sexual needs. If he is unsure of his masculinity, he may attempt to cover up or compensate for real or imagined deficiencies. He may display his insecurity by refusing sexual relations or accelerating sexual behavior. He may be afraid that you will reject his sexual advances or fear that he won't be able to adequately meet your sexual needs.

> Your husband may believe that his masculinity is tied in with his ability to satisfy your sexual needs.

You can help your husband avoid these fears if you realize that he has a greater physical and emotional challenge in sexual intercourse than you do. The success of the act depends primarily on his ability to obtain and maintain a strong erection. Support him by displaying your confidence in his sexual ability through word and deed. You may convey this by embracing him eagerly, kissing him warmly, or sighing in appreciation at the right time. Your actions should give the unmistakable impression that you can hardly wait to enjoy sex with him.

You may be thinking, *Am I supposed to pretend?* Since you know God planned this relationship for your mutual sexual enjoyment, pretending should never be necessary. Therefore, look at it as if you are simply anticipating your sexual excitement and communicate this eagerness to your husband. An effective way to give your husband pleasure is to let him know you care about him and desire to have intercourse with him. Should your words and actions be purely an act of faith, God can use your faith to bring them into present reality.

> Since you know God planned
> this relationship
> for your mutual sexual enjoyment,
> pretending should never be necessary.

WHEN YOUR HUSBAND IS DISINTERESTED

What if your husband is not interested in you sexually? Remember, a beautiful sexual relationship does not start when you go to bed. Sex is an expression of both your lives lived in an atmosphere of love. Ask Christ to show you if you have unintentionally been critical, cutting, sarcastic, or jealous or if you have implied that your husband's sexual abilities are inferior or inadequate for you. Perhaps you need to review the basics found in Chapter 11. Perhaps your husband is just too tired or under great stress. Often a wise counselor can help to pinpoint reasons behind sexual disinterest.

Joan tried to get her husband to go for a medical checkup, feeling his inability to have sexual relations with her was a physical problem. Although erectile dysfunction and depression, for example, can cause sexual disinterest, this wasn't true of Joan's husband. Finally he handed her an article he had clipped from the paper. It said, in essence, that a man does not find a woman sexually appealing if she is constantly bickering or has attacked his masculinity by not allowing him to be the leader, provider, and protector in his home. Unfortunately, Joan was not teachable in this area and did not respond to her husband's attempts to communicate his needs. Their marriage ended in divorce.

SEXUALITY AS A WEAPON

Never be guilty of using sex as a weapon, whether your goal is to punish your husband or get something from him. For example if you withhold your body in order to obtain something, you are prostituting yourself because you are exchanging your body for something you want. Remember, Paul wrote, *"The wife's body does not belong to her alone but also to her husband....Do not deprive each other..."* (1 Cor. 7:4-5). If you place a price tag on your sexual relationship, your husband may feel the price is too high and go shopping elsewhere. Or he may, in turn, erect physical and emotional walls that include anger and bitterness toward you.

POWERFUL CHILDHOOD EXPERIENCES

Sexual problems can also result if you or your husband has a warped idea of love, sex, or marriage because of childhood experiences. For instance, as a child you might have asked your mother, "Where do babies come from?"

Your mother may have replied, "Nice little girls don't ask such questions. When you get bigger, you will learn about such things."

Because of her attitude, you may have concluded that there is something bad about "where babies come from," and you did not question her further about such things. You may have gotten the rest of your sexual education in an atmosphere of secrecy, which caused you to feel sex was "dirty" rather than a beautiful, God-given expression of love in the context of marriage. If a parent's attitude or some unfortunate childhood experience has been the root of your resentments and sexual dysfunction, renounce your wrong feelings about sex. Accept God's forgiveness, allow Him to give you a positive and healthy reaction to sex, and—if necessary—seek counseling.

> ☺ If sexual abuse could be a source of your problems, find a godly counselor who can assist you and your spouse.

Sadly, many people today have been sexually abused, and some have a hard time even admitting this to themselves, much less a spouse or counselor. If sexual abuse could be a source of your problems, find a godly counselor who can assist you and your spouse.

LACK OF SEXUAL UNDERSTANDING

Maybe you are not satisfied sexually because your husband doesn't understand you. Even though the greater percentage of sexual "success" is a result of your attitude, it is my opinion that at least 20 percent depends on his education. He may not be aware that a woman is not usually sexually aroused as quickly as a man and needs tender words and longer foreplay before she is ready to enjoy orgasm. If this is true in your marriage, guide your husband gently, showing him actions and expressions that please you sexually.

> As you wholeheartedly desire
> to satisfy your husband sexually
> and respond positively to his actions,
> you will have increased sexual satisfaction.

When you respond to his efforts positively and with enthusiasm, he will be encouraged to make other efforts to please you. Let him know how much you enjoyed his efforts. If you did not have an orgasm, you can still respond positively. An orgasm is not always necessary for your lovemaking to be a pleasing experience. You will discover, however, that as you wholeheartedly desire to satisfy your husband sexually and respond positively to his actions, you will have increased sexual satisfaction.

TAKING SEXUAL INITIATIVE

Should you ever take initiative sexually? Certainly! When you do, any fears your husband has that you may reject him sexually will be dispelled immediately. Also, he will likely be stimulated by the idea that you find him sexually desirable. Many times a man's impotence is overcome by being near his turned-on wife. He is made aware of his sexual ability and is encouraged to enjoy intercourse. However, be careful not to become too aggressive in your sexual initiative.

If you become too aggressive and sexually demanding, your husband could be repulsed, feeling that he is not "the man in charge." Your sex life, as well as all other areas, must be balanced. When your husband's leadership in your home is not threatened, he will enjoy and be encouraged by times when you take sexual initiative.

DISTORTIONS OR ABUSES OF GOD'S PLAN FOR SEX

God has designed a complete, mutually satisfying, sexual relationship for you and your husband, so He has set certain boundaries or prohibitions because He loves you and desires you to be happy. Sex can be compared to another of God's good gifts—food. *"For everything God created is good, and nothing is to be rejected if it is received with thanksgiving, because it is consecrated by the word of God and prayer"* (1 Tim. 4:4-5). Food, when eaten in the proper proportions and balance, provides health and pleasure. But if we violate these boundaries, we can become gluttons. The sun, also God's gift, provides warmth and light, but can cause pain when we overexpose our skin to its rays. Likewise, the Bible gives a balanced, healthy view of sex. God does not hide the details, nor does He glamorize or glorify the wrong use of sex. God's information is complete and perfect!

For example, God has prohibited adultery (sex with someone other than your husband) because it destroys your soul oneness with your husband. The fact that adultery can destroy you as a person is revealed in Proverbs 6:32: *"Whoever commits adultery with a woman lacks understanding; He who does so destroys his own soul"* (NKJV).

God also says that sexual immorality affects the body: *"...All other sins a man commits are outside his body, but he who sins sexually sins against his own body"* (1 Cor. 6:18). Adultery can affect your body in many ways, such as causing you not to be able to function properly and taking away full enjoyment with your husband. Promiscuous sex also carries a huge risk of potentially life-threatening sexually transmitted infections and diseases. Furthermore, an adulterous person can become laden with guilt, shame, or distrust. As God clearly emphasizes, *"Marriage should be honored by all, and the marriage bed kept pure, for God will judge the adulterer and all the sexually immoral"* (Heb. 13:4). Without unity of soul, the sex act is an improper union of bodies and is not ultimately fulfilling.

Of course, adultery and promiscuity are not the only ways we distort God's plan for sex. Reading romance novels excessively, masturbating, daydreaming, fantasizing, pornography, engaging in an Internet relationship with a man who isn't your husband—all of these behaviors reflect an unwillingness to believe that God's way is best. They often stem from our own self-centeredness and lack of self-control.

While we may think of these activities as "harmless diversions," they are really "harmful distortions" because they shift the focus of our sexual desire from fulfilling our husbands' needs to fulfilling our own. This unbridled desire is lust, and because lust is not of God, it will never be satisfied. Not only that, if we indulge ourselves in this way, we risk becoming slaves to our own desires. When this happens, we violate the commands given to Christians in First Thessalonians 4:3

> *"For this is the will of God, that you should be consecrated (separated and set apart for pure and holy living): that you should abstain and shrink from all sexual vice"* (AMP)

> *"Beloved, I implore you…to abstain from the sensual urges (the evil desires, the passions of the flesh, your lower nature) that wage war against the soul"* (First (Peter 2:11 AMP).

Distortions or abuses of sex come from our sin nature or from satan himself. Satan masterfully distorts and counterfeits God's wonderful provision for us. Distortions will emphasize the body or sex without the soul relationship. When we enjoy sex according to God's plan, distortions and abuses of sex such as homosexuality, lesbianism, bestiality, wife-swapping, and pornographic activity will not be part of our lives.

Where such misuses have been a struggle, we find opportunity to grow in self-control. As we nurture this fruit of the Spirit and focus our desires on our spouse, we often find fulfillment in abundance and a deeper love for our mate. This is God's desire.

A Word About Forgiveness and Healing

Obviously I don't know what your specific marital situation is. But if you have been involved in immorality, remember that Jesus Christ paid for all our sins when He died on the cross. Confess your immorality as sin, accept Christ's forgiveness, and seek a life of fulfillment according to God's will.

Although God does forgive us of all our sins (see 1 John 1:9), usually we will still face great challenges if immorality has entered our marriages. Sexual sin creates a number of hidden and visible consequences, including deep emotional pain. So emotional healing can take quite a while, for instance. If some of the same factors that caused you (or your husband) to pursue sex outside of marriage remain unresolved, strife and unrest may continue.

> Sexual sin creates a number of hidden and visible consequences, including deep emotional pain.

Entire books have been written on the dynamics of putting a marriage back together after adultery (as well as sexual addictions), so I won't presume to explore this area now. I suggest, however, that you immediately seek out a trusted, wise, and godly counselor who is experienced in marital counseling. (Some counselors specialize in such areas as sexual addiction and helping people rebuild their lives and marriages after extramarital affairs.) Such a counselor can guide you to appropriate, Bible-based resources such as DVD's, seminars, and Christian books that can help you and your husband heal from the scars of immorality and build a new, stronger foundation for your marriage.

ENDNOTES

1. Some recommendations for books on physical fulfillment in marriage include:

- Dr. Ed Wheat and Gaye Wheat. *Intended for Pleasure.* (Grand Rapids MI:Fleming H. Revell, Co.)

- Tim LaHaye, *How to Be Happy Though Married.* Wheaton, IL. Tyndale House Publisher,.

- Michael Pearl, *Holy Sex,* No Greater Joy Ministries, Inc. 1000 Pearl Road, Pleasantville, Tn. 37147, 2002. www.NoGreaterJoy.org.

Conclusion

After 36 miraculous years of this book being in publication and 53 years of my marriage with DeWitt, this book is being revised, updated, and expanded. The foundational truths are the same. God's Word does not change. God has, however, expanded my insight and maturity in the application of these core truths in a few areas. Through the application of these truths, DeWitt and I find that our appreciation and love for each other grows daily. We have a closer unity than we ever believed possible. We are learning that you cannot limit God by our preconceived ideas and formulas. His creativity continues to amaze us as we allow Him to produce unity His way.

We are each learning to have our hunger and thirst satisfied by our own intimate love walk with Jesus (see John 6:35). As He is our portion (see Ps. 16:5), DeWitt and I are daily learning to enjoy and appreciate each other without requiring or expecting the other to be more than God made us to be. This enables us to say, "I'm a happy wife" and "I'm a happy husband" because the choice is ours.

My prayer is that you become the "happy wife" of a "happy husband." As this process develops, may the real woman you are in Christ not only stand up, but also move forward to release the fragrance of Christ to all those around you. This will enable you to fulfill Luke 21:19. *"By your steadfastness and patient endurance you shall win the true life of your souls"* (AMP). For me that is an adventure worth living my life for. It means that I want to fulfill my heavenly Father's purpose for my life while appropriating Jesus' provision on the cross, allowing me to accomplish my destiny. This will also produce an atmosphere for the same to happen in my mate's life as well as in the lives of those whom my life influences. Life's journey is about realizing that, while I am not yet perfect, as I walk with the Perfect One, He will draw others to Himself. Knowing Him and making Him known is therefore my focus.

If this is your prayerful desire, I come into agreement with you for a rich harvest in you, through you, and to all whom your life touches.

Readers' Guide to Personal or Group Reflection

God tells us in His Word that He has a plan for our lives—a good plan that will bring us a high level of satisfaction in all that we have and do. Yet, despite so many seeming advances in the positions women occupy in our society, many women feel dissatisfied and unhappy. It seems to me that it is becoming a national epidemic. How can we explain those contradictory ideas? More importantly, how can we begin to live life the way God planned for us from the beginning?

Darien Cooper has discovered the "secret" to living that satisfying life that God promised so long ago. She has lived it, and she has taught countless other women to experience that same level of contentment. But beware! This secret runs counter to almost everything we have been taught to believe in our 21st century culture.

Use the following questions for discussion in your group or as you think more deeply about the principles you have read in this book. You'll discover that God has in mind a system that was designed to bring maximum security, pleasure, and blessing to both men and women.

Is your marriage faltering? Are you or your husband considering divorce as the only possible solution? God can turn that around and restore the joy of your relationship.

Is your marriage "OK"—not what you expected, but you're getting along fairly well? God longs for you to experience the richness of a truly committed, godly marriage.

By applying God's principles for the marriage relationship, you can experience firsthand all the blessings and joy God intended to pour out on the human race through the family. Put His promise to the test and see if you don't discover that you really *can* be the happy wife of a happy husband.

CHAPTER 1—THE PERFECT PLAN

1. In a group setting, ask each woman to share her name, something about herself, and something about her marital journey.

2. Read aloud Ephesians 3:20 and John 10:10. Do you feel these verses apply to you and your family in your present experience? Why or why not? According to Isaiah 1:19, what is your part in bringing about God's will in your life? Discuss.

3. When did you become aware that God had a personal, detailed plan for your life? Are you still in the process of embracing this truth? Explain. Reread Psalm 139:13-18 aloud and discuss the application. How does it make you feel to know that God can work everything

together for good in your life? (See Romans 8:28.)

4. Share what the word *submission* has meant to you and how you formed your ideas. Does substituting the word *responder* give a different perspective? Read Ephesians 5:21. According to this verse, who is required to be subject to one another? Since your life is the only one you can change, where must your focus be?

5. Did you change in the way you related to your husband after you were married as compared to while you were dating (i.e., going places with him, being polite and grateful for what he did, looking nice for him, and so forth)? Why or why not?

6. Do happy marriages automatically happen or must they be built? Read Proverbs 14:1. Do you feel that you have been a wise woman or a foolish woman in regard to your responses in your marriage? What specific things can you do to change past foolish actions?

7. Do you feel that adequate training is provided for most couples prior to marriage? If not,

how can this be improved? What steps are you willing to take to make this happen?

Chapter 2—Your Relationship With the Designer

1. After reading Genesis 2:1-18, describe Adam's life before Eve was created. Why do you think God said in verse 18 that Adam needed a helpmate?

2. Have you witnessed the influence that a woman can have on a man? Explain. Discuss the influence that Eve had on Adam in Genesis 3:1-6. How could it have been different?

3. Discuss the influence that Sarai had on her husband, as recorded in Genesis 16. What seemed to be the motivating factor behind Sarai's actions? Share times that you have likewise been caught in the same trap.

4. What is the source of the searching, restlessness, or void that all of us feel in our lives? What have you used to try to fill this void? Explain your journey.

5. How is the universal void in all of us filled? When did you come to know Jesus Christ as your Savior, or are you still in the process? Share your experience.

6. Once you have received Jesus Christ as your personal Savior, how can you know that you are God's child? (See 1 John 5:11-13.)

7. Once you become a Christian, is it possible to once again take control of your life? Explain how Second Corinthians 9:8, Romans 8:28-29, Ephesians 2:10, and First John 1:9 work together to help us in our journey in becoming like Christ.

8. Share your greatest struggle at this time and what God is showing you.

9. Compare Christianity and marriage. What areas do you see that need to be improved upon in both your walk with Jesus and your relationship with your mate? What steps will you make this coming week?

CHAPTER 3—HELPING YOUR HUSBAND LOVE HIMSELF

1. Which of the following truths do you have the hardest time embracing? God says that you: are a person of great worth and value; belong to His royal family with a great heritage possible; are accepted and loved unconditionally; and will have all your needs supplied by Him. Ask Him to make the truths that seem unreal to you a present reality. Which of the above do you have the hardest time realizing is true for your mate? Why? Ask God to help you to see your mate as He does.

2. When were you the most encouraged by someone's complimenting words? How did it change your day's experience? Could your words do the same for your mate?

3. Read Ephesians 5:33, Hebrews 10:24, First Thessalonians 5:11, and Proverbs 3:27. Remember that sincere, genuine compliments create an environment that allows others to taste of God's love, making it easier for them to yield completely to His leadership in their lives. What did you admire in your mate when

you were dating? Do you still see those qualities? Explain.

_____

_____

4. Over the next several days, keep a journal
   listing positive qualities you observe in your
   mate as you watch what he does, listen to him
   talk, and join him in things that interest him.
   Ask God to open your eyes to traits you have
   forgotten or have never seen. Begin to weave
   these insights into your conversation in a natural way. After doing this, what difference do
   you sense in him and yourself?

_____

_____

5. What must be your motive in encouraging
   your mate? (See Colossians 3:23-24.) What
   has been your past motivation? Explain. Ask
   God to purify your goals for living.

_____

_____

6. As you fulfill your role of encourager, keep in
   mind that you are not your mate's total driving force. Jesus wants to be. We are simply
   His vessels carrying His love. Read Galatians
   6:7-10. What jumps out to you in these Scriptures? Ask God to completely develop these
   insights in your life.

_____

_____

_____

7. What does God promise in First Corinthians 15:58? How does this encourage you? Explain.

Chapter 4—Accepting Your Husband as He Is

1. What surprises did you experience in your mate after the exchange of "I dos"? What were your mate's surprises concerning you? If you do not know, ask.

2. How does Christ accept us? Read Romans 5:8; 15:7 and Ephesians 2:8-9. How should we respond to our mates in light of this truth? What is your initial reaction to this concept? Ask God to be your power though which this is accomplished.

3. Read First Corinthians 13:4-7 and personalize it by putting your name in the place of the word *love*. Ask Jesus to be your power as you respond in this way.

4. What expectations have you had concerning your mate that have been dashed? (See First Peter 2:6; Psalm 62:5.) Ask Jesus to meet your

inner needs as you fellowship with Him and to guide you in creating a climate of acceptance throughout your home.

5. Read Proverbs 16:25 and list some things that you might be doing that seem right to you, but may actually be the ways of death— death to intimacy, death to another person's self-image, death to a good marriage? Read John 16:8-11. Who can you trust to take care of your mate?

6. Do you give unasked-for advice? Why? We are to speak the truth in love, but what must we guard against? What is your biggest temptation? What helps you in this regard? Explain.

7. What traits attracted you to your mate? What traits are irritating to you now? Discuss how these irritations can be channeled in the right direction.

8. Acceptance does not mean that you approve of, tolerate, or encourage carnal ways. Why would doing so be destructive to you? To your husband? To your marriage?

9. Read Philippians 4:6-8. List and give to God troubling attitudes, actions, and habits. Then thank God for everything that is good, lovely, and honorable. Expect His peace to follow. Discuss helpful insights or successes in doing the above assignment.

CHAPTER 5—NOT SECOND BEST

1. At the time of marriage, you and your mate became one or "one flesh" (see Gen. 2:24). Ask God to show you any actions or attitudes of disloyalty, selfishness, jealousy, or bossiness on your part that has hindered the bonding that God wants to do. As you make your list (take your time on each area), discuss why these things have happened and what you can do to correct them.

2. Compare your life and marriage to the wheel of proper balance. Carefully review each spoke.

3. Do you think your husband feels like your home is his palace—a haven where he can be himself? Why or why not? What can you change?

4. Do you have a hard time knowing when to serve the children or your husband? Explain.

5. Are finances a strain? How can each of your strengths compliment the other's weaknesses to correct this? Discuss this issue, being willing to face any fears and resting in the truth in Philippians 4:19.

6. Are there any areas of strain or victory with in-laws? Read Ephesians 5:31 and discuss any areas where you or your mate have not left your family of origin. How can you begin to correct this?

7. Living purposefully, as Ephesians 5:15-17 says, is easier for some than others. Evaluate the following areas of your life in regard to purposeful living: (1) personal relationship with Jesus Christ, (2) husband, (3) children, (4) personal grooming and rest, (5) household responsibilities, and (6) outside activities. What changes need to be made? What steps will you take this week?

8. How responsible have you felt for your husband's spirituality? Read First Corinthians

3:6-7; 7:16 and John 6:35. Consider your responsibility.

9. Examine your family relationships to see if there is anyone whom you have put in God's place. If a name comes to mind, ask God's forgiveness. Ask Him to show you how to lovingly untangle the wrong relationships and for strength to do so.

10. Embrace any areas of change that God shows you, knowing that His revelation is for the purpose of healing and restoring you to the person He designed you to be before sin brought pain from wrong living. Apply First John 1:9. Rejoice in another spiritual bath! Praise God that He loves you just as you are, but too much to leave you that way!

Chapter 6—Follow the Leader

1. Carefully read Ephesians 5:22-23. What rises up within you when you read this Scripture? Are there any negative feelings associated with this divine order? Examine them. Do they come from what you have seen modeled or from past pain? Could they be from a misunderstanding of God's divine order? Ask God to give you His perspective.

2. Meditate on First Corinthians 11:3. What was Jesus' role to the Father while on earth? Was this beneficial or destructive? How does the Church obey Christ? How are these roles like our relationship to our mates? List inappropriate applications in your marital roles. Describe ways these can be adjusted.

3. Discuss the differences in the male and female roles, gifts, and temperaments and how God designed these to complete each other rather than be competitive. What new insights do you have that can help make your marriage flow more smoothly? List specifics to begin applying.

4. Compare the marital roles in your marriage to those of a president and vice president of a company. Are there areas that need to be adjusted? What can you do to start the transition?

5. Your advice and insights are critical to your partner's wise decisions. Appropriate sharing will not be by giving advice on a man-to-man

basis, an attitude of authority, superiority, or motherliness, or by trying to force your point of view on your mate. Read Proverbs 31:11-12, 26. What characterizes your advice-giving? Why? Discuss ways to improve your times of sharing.

6. Because God's plan for the home is outlined in God's Word, who are you really looking to when you look to your husband for leadership? Read Romans 8:32, Psalm 84:11, and Jeremiah 29:11. Let Him comfort you and quiet any reservations you might have about His plan for marriage.

7. Why is staying under God's umbrella of protection through a submissive spirit so critical? Read Romans 13:1-5, with special attention on verse 5. Then compare this passage with Ephesians 4:26-27 to form your conclusion.

Chapter 7—Protection for Your Benefit

1. Describe the ways in which you have enjoyed your husband's physical protection. In what areas would you like to experience his protection? Why do you feel this is important or unimportant? Discuss contributing factors, positively and negatively.

2. Whose responsibility is it to provide financially for the family? See Genesis 3:17-19 and First Timothy 5:8. What was your experience in your family of origin?

3. When a woman complements the family finances (see Prov. 31:13-14, 24), what questions should she ask to keep her activities balanced? Have you seen this modeled?

4. Describe how a woman's gifts and sensitivity can help the man be a more productive provider. How does this apply to your marriage? Would you like to grow in this area?

5. How has your mate protected you psychologically and emotionally? What would you like for him to do differently? What steps can you take to point your marriage in that direction?

6. Our attitude toward our mate reveals our spiritual condition. Read Psalm 139:23-24 and ask God to reveal any attitudes you need

to release for change as you take the positive steps in that direction.

7. In what areas have you assumed your husband's role? Make a list along with a plan for correction. Ask your husband's forgiveness for usurping his leadership role. Commit to supporting him in the future.

CHAPTER 8—GOD'S BEST FOR YOU

1. Do you want God's best? Before you answer, read Psalm 147:11 and John 10:10.

2. The mystery of the Christian life parallels the mystery of marital relationships. Read Ephesians 5:21-33, emphasizing verse 32 and comparing it with John 12:24-26. Discuss the parallels, both the aspects that are comforting and the parts that are frightening.

3. What does having a submissive spirit mean? Review the description in this chapter before completing your answer. What part does one's attitude play in a submissive spirit? What has been your previous and present understanding of submission? Explain.

4. Is submission only for women? Read Ephesians 5:21. Explain how the woman expresses her submissive spirit and how the man expresses a submissive spirit according to Ephesians 5:22-23. Whose role must we focus on? Why?

5. Share positive experiences you have had when deferring to your husband with a sweet attitude in a difficult situation. How was your faith in God increased as you saw Him work?

6. Does submission always mean obedience? See the story in Daniel 3:16-30. We must not disobey God's written Word or our conscience, but we can refuse with a submissive spirit. Give examples and discuss creative means of addressing a mate's need rather than a surface attitude.

7. Have you seen God intervene when you left the results in His hands and deferred to your husband, trusting God to "Romans 8:28" the situation? Explain.

8. What does it mean to respect your husband's position, not necessarily his personality or actions? How have you been able to implement this? Describe what it did for you and your mate.

CHAPTER 9—TIMELESS BEAUTY

1. What determines one's beauty? See First Peter 3:4 and Proverbs 23:7. What kind of beauty is your heritage as a child of God? (See Proverbs 31:25.) What have been your emphases in order to make yourself more beautiful? Describe any area in which your focus has been wrong.

---

2. In Christ's physical absence from earth, describe three major means that God uses to conform us to His likeness. (See Psalm 119:11,97,114,130,133; John 16:13; 1 Thessalonians 5:17; John 16:24.) In which area are you the strongest? Weakest? Discuss plans for improving your weak areas.

---

3. Of the deadly traps that mar your beauty— anger, fear, and depression—which do you struggle with most? Or how do you react when things do not go the way that you want or anticipate? How do these mar your inner

and outward beauty? Describe evidences you have observed in your life and in others.

4. Times of disappointment and disillusionment should be occasions for reevaluating who and what we are looking to for fulfillment. Describe your most frequent disappointment. Read First Peter 2:6, Psalm 62:5, and Proverbs 4:23-27. Another person's sin can cause us displeasure, but what is the only change for which we are responsible? Recommit your ways to Him.

5. When your faults or others' faults become your focus, it is easy to become angry, fearful, or depressed. How do the following Scriptures challenge us to refocus? Read Colossians 3:1-3; Second Corinthians 5:17; Ephesians 4:22-32; and Galatians 2:20. What insights are you seeing that will help in the future? Praise Him for His guidance and strength to become more like Him each day.

Chapter 10—How to Handle Problems and Trials

1. How did Adam and Eve respond when they sinned? Read Genesis 3:7-13. What should be our response according to Proverbs 28:13?

How did you handle the last time you or your mate made a mistake? Read Proverbs 17:9 and 20:22 and discuss ways of handling similar situations in the future.

2. Contention and strife happen in everyone's life. How is it normally handled in your family? What is the solution according to God's Word? (See Matthew 5:25; Proverbs 17:14; 18:19.) Discuss steps you can take when strife happens in the future.

3. Criticism is often hard to accept unless we remember truths from Proverbs 23:12; 29:1; and 25:12. How can this help the next time you are criticized?

4. How do you naturally respond to hurtful remarks from your mate? Discuss the different facets involved in dealing with such unpleasantness: (1) ask for clarification, (2) share your feelings in love at an appropriate time, (3) cover with love and forgiveness, and (4) leave it in God's hands. Which of the four is hardest for you do you? Ask God to make you sensitive to respond as He directs in future situations.

5. Which is harder for you, to not have your mate's praise or to gracefully handle praise? Discuss the insights given in Proverbs 25:27; 4:8; 3:3-4; and 27:21. Describe future reactions that would please God and be beneficial to you.

---

6. Is there an area of your life that is hard to completely surrender to God? Read Psalm 138:7-8. In light of His Word, will you by faith give Him this area and thank Him for how He will work it out?

---

7. What area or situation in your life have you had difficulty thanking God for? Read First Thessalonians 5:18 and Romans 8:28. You are to thank Him that He will use it for good and strengthen you as He builds your character to bring forth His likeness. What can you release to Him now in faith through thanksgiving? Thanksgiving is the breath of life! Breathe deeply!

CHAPTER 11—REVIEWING BEAUTY BASICS

1. Since a Christian's body is the temple of the Holy Spirit, we should give it the appropriate care. (See 1 Corinthians 6:19-20.) Have you been aware of this truth? How does it make

you feel? What difference should it make in your life?

2. Ask God to give you insight as to how you can be a better caregiver of your body. Start with your diet. Are you eating healthy foods? Are you eating too much? Not enough? Make a plan and cooperate with His Spirit as He directs you.

3. Are you helping your body to be strong by giving it the proper balance of exercise and rest? Which is more difficult, getting adequate rest or adequate exercise? What can you do to correct any imbalance?

4. Ask God to show you any areas that He wants you to work on concerning your makeup, hair, or hygiene. Prepare to carry them out.

5. How can you represent Christ more effectively through your clothing and posture? Go to others for help if you need to. Write out what God is showing you.

6. Which of the above (in questions 2-5) is easiest for you to neglect? Take steps this week to begin the needed changes. Treat yourself. You are royalty and worth it!

Chapter 12—Sexual Fulfillment in Your Marriage

1. Whose idea was sex? (See Genesis 1:27-31; 2:18,24.) Would God call something good that was not good?

---

2. How do you know that it is God's will for you to enjoy your sexual relationship with your husband? (See Proverbs 5:15-19; Hebrews 13:4.) Describe your past feelings about sex. Where were they formed? Replace any false perspective with God's perspective as you meditate upon His Word and give your wrong conceptions to Him for healing and restoration. Respond to your husband by faith, seeking to bring pleasure to Him, and let God's grace be sufficient for your healing as you respond appropriately.

---

3. The enemy does not create anything, but only distorts that which our Lord creates. What are some ways that satan has distorted and abused sex? Name some ways that you can begin to correct such distortions and abuses.

4. Sexual problems in marriage can result from many sources. Can you identify with any of the following: ignorance of male and female sexual differences, improperly solving other problems, poor timing, lack of honest communication, using sex as a weapon to punish your mate, warped ideas of sex from one's past, lack of consideration for your mate's needs, or lack of proper preparation. Have any of these played a role in your marriage? Explain. Read James 1:5 and ask the Lord to give you wisdom to take the next step in correcting any problem areas.

5. Read First Corinthians 7:1-5 and Proverbs 31:22. Make plans for adding "newness" to your marriage by saying and doing the unexpected with eager anticipation of the delight God wants you to experience with your mate.

6. God ordained marriage to reflect your relationship with Him. Let Him use your marriage to cause you to fall in love with Him and each other more deeply each day! How are you beginning to see this happen? What areas can you trust Him to begin working on today?

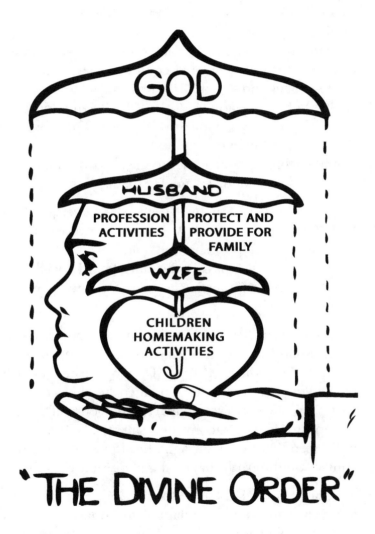

"THE DIVINE ORDER"

About Darien Cooper

Darien Cooper is the wife of DeWitt, a retired construction contractor. They have three married sons—Craig, Brian, and Ken—and 12 grandchildren. A resident of Ringgold, Georgia, Darien's practical teaching on the woman's role in marriage and complete abandonment to Jesus Christ has changed countless lives both in the United States and abroad. Her teaching series "You Can Be the Wife of a Happy Husband" has been a source of great help to those women who have put into practice the biblical principles. Says one, "Application of these truths has brought me closer to my husband than we've been in 11 years of marriage. He thanks you, too."

A graduate of Carson Newman College, Jefferson City, Tennessee, with a B.A. in sociology, Darien Cooper hoped to help others find solutions to life's problems. Though she passed the state board social work examinations, circumstances prevented her from entering that field.

Some years later, while serving temporarily with her husband as associate staff of the Lay Ministry of Campus Crusade for Christ, Darien learned biblical principles that completely changed her life and marriage. "We were growning apart until God enabled me to apply these truths to my life," she says. DeWitt was so impressed that he encouraged her to begin teaching a course "on the truth that changed our marriage."

The "Happy Husband" lecture series has been extensively reworked and adapted to book form in the hope that you will find God's greatest happiness by applying His principles to your marriage. Though the book is designed for your individual help and enrichment, it is ideal for group study as well.

A CD course, DVD, and other materials based on this book, and other subjects by the author, are available by writing His Way Library, P.O.Box 954, Rocky Face, GA 30740. They are also available from Darien's Website: www.darienbcooper.com.

In the right hands, This Book will Change Lives!

Most of the people who need this message will not be looking for this book. To change their lives, you need to put a copy of this book in their hands.

> *But others (seeds) fell into good ground, and brought forth fruit, some a hundred-fold, some sixty-fold, some thirty-fold* (Matthew 13:8).

Our ministry is constantly seeking methods to find the good ground, the people who need this anointed message to change their lives. Will you help us reach these people?

> *Remember this—a farmer who plants only a few seeds will get a small crop. But the one who plants generously will get a generous crop* (2 Corinthians 9:6).

EXTEND THIS MINISTRY BY SOWING
3 BOOKS, 5 BOOKS, 10 BOOKS, OR MORE TODAY,
AND BECOME A LIFE CHANGER!

Thank you,

Don Nori Sr., Publisher
Destiny Image
Since 1982